D0841854

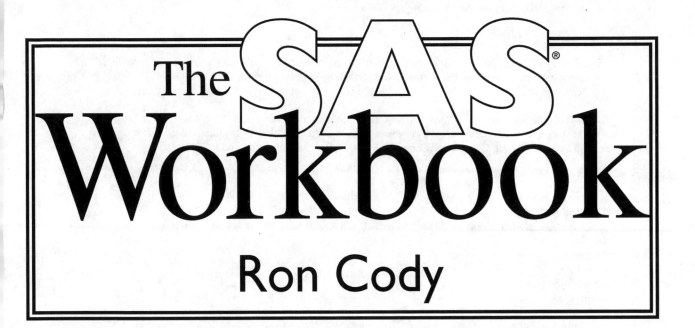

The SAS® Workbook

Ron Cody

SAS Publishing
Books by Users Press

Table of Contents

SECTION 3 • SAS® Programming Techniques

SECTION 4 • Statistics Problems

SECTION 5 • SAS® Puzzles to Test Your Skills

SECTION 6 • Appendix

Preface

The SAS Workbook and *The SAS Workbook Solutions* are collections of SAS programming problems and solutions, respectively, grouped by topic. The problems should be useful for individuals wanting to improve their skills, for classes in SAS programming, and for those attending problem sessions associated with SAS workshops.

Although books, manuals, and workshops are all useful mechanisms for learning and improving your SAS programming skills, one of the best ways to transfer this information into actual programming skills is by writing lots and lots and lots and lots (OK, you get the idea) of programs.

The problems in this book have been carefully selected to include many of the same techniques that are needed in typical SAS applications such as cleaning "dirty" data, using arrays, or working with SAS dates. I include problems that I have encountered in my over 17 years of SAS programming.

Each problem is organized with a Tools list that suggests SAS statements or procedures that may be useful in solving the problem. Several references that you may find useful include

- *SAS Procedures Guide, Version 6, Third Edition*

- *SAS Language: Reference , Version 6, First Edition*

- *SAS Programming by Example*

- *SAS Language and Procedures: Usage, Version 6, First Edition*

- *SAS Language and Procedures: Usage 2, Version 6, First Edition*

- SAS Technical Report P-222, *Changes and Enhancements to Base SAS Software, Release 6.07*

All of these reference sources are available from SAS Institute in Cary, North Carolina.

Following the Tools list, each problem provides you with sample data or refers you to a data file or a SAS data set described in the Appendix.

The problems in the Statistics Problems section are intended to be used by students in a basic or intermediate level statistics course or by researchers wishing to improve their skills in solving statistical problems. These problems have been kept separate so as not to frighten those who use the SAS System for mostly non-statistical applications.

Once you have worked out, or at least attempted, a problem, it's time to look at the book's solution. You may or may not have been able to solve the problem. If you did solve the problem, your solution may differ. If not, you will benefit from seeing the solution now that you have spent some time in trying to solve it yourself. Don't think that the book's solutions are necessarily superior to yours. The SAS language has so many powerful programming tools that most problems can be solved in many different ways.

The solutions listed in *The SAS Workbook Solutions* assume that all external raw data files are located in a subdirectory called WORKBOOK on the C: drive of a microcomputer. You may substitute the appropriate file description for the operating environment you are using. Descriptions of these files, listings of their contents, and a program to create the SAS data set CLINICAL are located in the Appendix.

You may wonder why there is a separate solutions book. It is the nature of SAS programming (actually most computer programming) that once you are shown the solution to a problem, the learning potential of the problem is lost. You think that the solution is obvious once you see it, even though it would have taken considerable effort for you to have written it yourself. And it is through this effort that you become a better programmer.

I therefore removed the temptation for students to flip to the back of the book and take a quick peek at the solutions. Instructors may also feel more comfortable in assigning problems without the solutions too close at hand.

The SAS Workbook Solutions contains one or more solutions to each of the problems. Some of the lines are commented, but most of the solutions do not contain extensive explanations. The two books together should be useful as a reference tool as well.

I hope you improve your programming skills and have fun in the process.

RPC

Spring 1996

Acknowledgments

This is the fun part. The book is almost finished and I get to thank all the people who helped. Since this is my second book published by SAS Institute, I must enjoy working with them--and I do. I can't say enough good things about the publications group at SAS Institute. They are terrific. They maintain a high level of professionalism yet are gentle and kind with authors like me who make lots of silly mistakes.

I wish to thank all the folks at SAS Institute who helped transform this work from manuscript to book in record time. As always, special thanks to David Baggett for his encouragement and good cheer. Although I don't know all the names, I wish to thank the reviewers for their constructive suggestions and for catching a number of programming errors. Caroline Brickley deserves special credit for coordinating the first edit pass. Thanks to Joan M. Stout for her very careful detail editing and for finding some very subtle mistakes. I have not spoken with all the production staff but there are numerous tasks that go on "behind the scenes" that are vital. Therefore, my thanks to the production specialists Blanche W. Phillips, Denise T. Jones, and Candy R. Farrell. Also, for the creative artist who designed the cover, thanks to Ellen Hood for a great job.

Finally, thanks to my wife, Jan, and my two boys, Russ and Preston, for their support and encouragement.

Ron Cody
Spring, 1996

SECTION 1   DATA Step Programming

CHAPTERS

CHAPTER 1   Inputting Raw Data

PROBLEMS

INTRODUCTION

This chapter contains problems on reading raw data with an INPUT statement. All the problems read "instream" data, that is, data that you submit as part of your program. However, all the techniques used here can also be applied to reading data from external files (discussed in Chapter 2). For those "old-timers" who like to use a CARDS statement, you may still do so. The newer term DATALINES is equivalent and is used throughout this book.

PROBLEM 1
Reading Data Values Separated by Spaces

Tools

INPUT statement

PROC PRINT

Data

You have collected some data on a group of students. The data values, separated by one or more spaces, represent the variables F_Name (first name), ID, Gender, GPA (grade point average), Height and Weight.

Hector	123	M	3.5	59	155
Nancy	328	F	3.7	52	99
Edward	747	M	2.4	62	205
Michelle	778	F	3.0	54	115
Sampson	289	M	3.5	60	180

Directions

Create a temporary SAS data set called CLASS from these lines of data. Include the lines of data "instream" in the program. Display the contents of this data set.

Notes

1. All the first names are 8 characters or less.

2. ID is to be stored as character data.

PROBLEM 2
Reading Data Values, Including Missing Values, Separated by Spaces

Tools

INPUT statement

Data

Raw data similar to Problem 1 with some missing values

Hector	123	M	3.5	.	155
.	328	F	3.7	52	99
Edward	747	.	.	.	.
Michelle	778	F	3.0	54	.
Sampson	289	M	3.5	60	180

Directions

Repeat Problem 1 with the modified data. Note that there are several missing values (both for numeric and character variables) which are represented by periods.

PROBLEM 3

Reading Data Values Separated by Spaces with a Character Value Greater than 8 Bytes Long

Tools

> INPUT statement
>> Colon format modifier (:) or
> LENGTH statement or
> INFORMAT statement

Data

Raw data similar to Problem 1 with one name greater than 8 characters in length

Hector	123	M	3.5	59	155
Nancy	328	F	3.7	52	99
Edward	747	M	2.4	62	205
Michelle	778	F	3.0	54	115
Washington	289	M	3.5	60	180

Directions

Repeat Problem 1 with the new data. Note that one of the names is now longer than 8 characters long.

PROBLEM 4

Reading Data Values Where Missing Values Are Represented by Periods except at the End of Short Data Lines

Tools

> INFILE statement
>> MISSOVER option
> INPUT statement

Data

Raw data similar to Problem 1 with some missing values and short records

```
Hector      123     M       3.5     .       155
.           328     F       3.7     52      99
Edward      747
Michelle    778     F       3.0     54
Sampson     289     M       3.5     60      180
```

Directions

Repeat Problem 1 with the new data. Note that there are several missing values (both for numeric and character variables) and there are some short records.

PROBLEM 5

Reading Data Values Separated by Commas Where Missing Values Are Represented by Two Adjacent Commas and Some of the Character Values Are Placed in Double Quotes

---

Tools

> INFILE statement
> > DSD option
>
> INPUT statement

Data

Raw data similar to Problem 1 with comma delimiters

```
Hector,123,M,3.5,,155
,328,"F",3.7,52,99
"Edward",747,,,,
Michelle,778,F,3.0,54,,
Sampson,289,M,3.5,60,180
```

Directions

Repeat Problem 1 using comma-delimited data. Note that some of the character values are enclosed in double quotes and that consecutive commas (without any space between) represent missing values.

PROBLEM 6
Reading Data Values Using Starting and Ending Column Numbers

Tools
INPUT statement, with column numbers

Data
Raw data similar to Problem 1 lined up in columns

```
            1         2         3         4         5
  1234567890123456789012345678901234567890123456789012
  --------------------------------------------------------
  Hector      123     M       3.5     59        155
  Nancy       328     F       3.7     52         99
  Edward      747     M       2.4     62        205
  Michelle    778     F       3.0     54        115
  Sampson     289     M       3.5     60        180
```

Directions
Use the same data as in Problem 1, but this time write the INPUT statement using starting and ending column numbers. The data are listed with column numbers displayed.

PROBLEM 7
Reading Data Values with Missing Character and Numeric Values Using Starting and Ending Column Numbers

Tools
INFILE statement
   PAD option
INPUT statement, with column numbers

Data
Raw data similar to Problem 1 lined up in columns with some missing values and short records

```
            1         2         3         4         5
  1234567890123456789012345678901234567890123456789012
  --------------------------------------------------------
  Hector      123     M       3.5               155
              328     F       3.7     52         99
  Edward      747
  Michelle    778     F       3.0     54
  Sampson     289     M       3.5     60        180
```

Directions

Repeat Problem 6 with the modified data. Note that there are now blanks representing both character and numeric missing values. Notice that lines 3 and 4 are short records that are not padded with blanks.

PROBLEM 8
Reading Data Values Using Pointers and Informats

Tools

INPUT statement, with column pointers (@) and informats

Data

The same raw data as in Problem 6

Directions

Instead of using starting and ending column numbers for the data values (as in Problem 6), use column pointers and informats to read the same data values and create a SAS data set called CLASS. Use the data description that follows to help you write the INPUT statement:

Variable	Starting Column	Length	Type
F_NAME	1	8	Char
ID	13	3	Char
GENDER	22	1	Char
GPA	31	3	Numeric
HEIGHT	39	2	Numeric
WEIGHT	49	3	Numeric

PROBLEM 9
Reading Mixed Record Types in One DATA Step

Tools

INPUT statement, single trailing at sign (@)

Data

Survey data as shown

```
          1         2
12345678901234567890
--------------------
001MRY 3     1994
00923FDY 1   1995
012FDN 2     1994
00518MRN 2   1995
003MDY 4     1994
```

Directions

You have data from a survey administered in 1994 and 1995. In 1995, it was decided to record the age of each person (which was not done in 1994). Age information was not added at the end of the raw data. Instead, it was placed right after the subject ID, creating two completely different data layouts for the two years. Fortunately, the year the survey was administered was also entered into the data file. Create a temporary SAS data set called SURVEY which correctly reads these mixed records. The data description follows:

1994 Data Description

Variable	Description	Starting Column	Ending Column	Format
ID	Subject ID	1	3	Char
GENDER	Subject Gender	4	4	Char
PARTY	Political Party	5	5	Char
VOTE	Did you vote in the last election?	6	6	Char
NUM_TV	Number of TV's	7	8	Numeric
YEAR	Survey year	15	18	Char

1995 Data Description

Variable	Description	Starting Column	Ending Column	Format
ID	Subject ID	1	3	Char
AGE	Subject's age	4	5	Numeric
GENDER	Subject Gender	6	6	Char
PARTY	Political Party	7	7	Char
VOTE	Did you vote in the last election?	8	8	Char
NUM_TV	Number of TV's	9	10	Numeric
YEAR	Survey year	15	18	Char

PROBLEM 10
Creating a Single Observation from More than One Line of Raw Data

Tools

INPUT statement, line and column pointers (# and @), informats

Data

Car survey data as follows

```
          1         2         3         4         5
12345678901234567890123456789012345678901234567890
--------------------------------------------------
12310/21/46             NJ             08822
123 2      Ford      Oldsmobile
23711/01/55             NY             11518
237 1      Chevy
```

Directions

A survey was conducted and the data were recorded using two lines of data for each subject. Use the data description and sample lines of data to create a SAS data set called SURVEY, with one observation per subject. The file description follows:

	Variable	Description	Starting Column	Ending Column	Type
Line 1	SUBJECT	Subject number	1	3	Char
	DOB	Date of Birth	4	11	MM/DD/YY
	STATE	State where living	25	26	Char
	ZIP_CODE	Zip Code	40	44	Character
Line 2	SUBJECT	Subject number	1	3	Char
	NUMBER	Number of cars	5	5	Numeric
	CAR1	Make of Car 1	11	20	Char
	CAR2	Make of Car 2	21	30	Char

Notes

1. You may use either pointers and informats for all of your variables, or you may use column specifications for all of your variables except for DOB for which you will need either a pointer and an informat or an INFORMAT statement.

2. For this problem, do not read the SUBJECT value in line 2 of the data. In a more sophisticated program, you might want to read this as a different variable and check that it is the same as the subject number in line 1.

PROBLEM 11

Creating More than One Observation from a Single Data Line

Tools

INPUT statement, double trailing at sign (@@)

Data

Twenty temperatures as shown

```
21   23    29 33 19   28
33   39 43   44 28   21 24     27  29
37   32    31   33 29
```

Directions

A researcher collected 20 temperatures (one for each day) and entered them on several lines as shown in the data section.

As you can see, there are several temperatures per line (not always the same number) and there are one or more spaces between each number. Create a temporary SAS data set called TEMPER from these data. Print out the contents of this data set.

PROBLEM 12

Creating More than One Observation from a Single Data Line (Two Variables)

Tools

INPUT statement, double trailing at sign (@@)

Data

Twenty pairs of days of the month and temperatures as shown

```
5 21   6   23    7   29 8 33 9 19   10   28
11   33   12   39 13   43   14     44 15 28   16 21 17 24     18 27 19   29
20 37   21 32   22   31 23 33   24 29
```

Directions

This time the researcher recorded the day of the month along with each of the temperatures and entered them in pairs (day temperature). Create a temporary SAS data set called TEMP_DAY containing two variables (DAY and TEMP), using these data. List the contents of this data set.

PROBLEM 13

Creating More than One Observation from a Single Data Line (Two Variables: One Character, One Numeric)

Tools

INPUT statement, double trailing at sign (@@)

Data

Rat data (GROUP and WEIGHT) in pairs with a varying number of pairs per line as shown

```
A 34   B 58    A 28   C 55
C 56   A 27    B 52   C 58   A 21   B 62
```

Directions

A researcher treated three groups of rats (Groups A, B, and C) and recorded the weight of each rat after one week. The data were arranged with each GROUP and WEIGHT in pairs, with a varying number of pairs on each line.

Write a SAS DATA step to read these data and create a temporary data set called RATS. Print out the contents of this data set.

PROBLEM 14

Reading "Free-form" Data, Creating More than One Observation from a Single Data Line

Tools

RETAIN statement
INPUT statement, double trailing at sign (@@)

Data

Rat data similar to Problem 13

```
A 34   28    B 58   52
62  C 55     A 27 21
C  56   58
```

Directions

The same data values as found in Problem 13 were entered differently. This time, the researcher entered a GROUP value (A, B, or C) followed by one or more weights as shown.

Write a SAS DATA step to read these data. Print out the contents of the data set. Again, call the data set RATS.

Hint

Look carefully at the tools needed for this problem.

PROBLEM 15

Using Variable Lists and Informat Lists to Make the INPUT Statement More Compact

Tools

INPUT statement, variable lists, and informat lists

Data

Instream data lines in the program to be rewritten

Directions

Rewrite the DATA step below, substituting an INPUT statement which uses a variable list and an informat list to make it more compact. Print out the contents of the data set.

```
DATA VARLIST;
    INPUT @1 Q1 2. @3 Q2 2. @5 Q3 2. @7 Q4 2. @9 Q5 2.
          @15 DATE1 MMDDYY8.
          @23 DATE2 MMDDYY8.
          @31 DATE3 MMDDYY8.
          @50 X1 $1. @51 X2 $1. @52 X3 $1.
          @53 Y1 $1. @54 Y2 $1. @55 Y3 $1.;
DATALINES;
1122334455    10/21/4611/13/4206/05/48        123456
9672347656    01/01/9501/02/9501/03/95        987654
;
```

PROBLEM 16

Using Variable Lists, Informat Lists, and Relative Column Pointers to Read Data Values

Tools

INPUT statement, variable lists, and informat lists; relative column pointers (+)

Data

Instream data lines in the program to be rewritten

Directions

Rewrite the DATA step below, substituting an INPUT statement which uses a variable list, an informat list, and relative column pointers (+). Print out the contents of the data set.

Hint

Read all the X's first, then the Y's, and finally, the Z's.

```
DATA POINTER;
   INPUT @1  X1 2.
         @3  Y1 2.
         @5  Z1 $3.
         @8  X2 2.
         @10 Y2 2.
         @12 Z2 $3.
         @15 X3 2.
         @17 Y3 2.
         @19 Z3 $3.;
DATALINES;
0102AAA0304BBB0506CCC
2837ABC9676DEF8765GHI
;
```

CHAPTER 2

Reading and Writing from External Files

INTRODUCTION

Problems in this chapter ask you to read data from external files. Since the specification for these files may vary from one operating environment to another, feel free to specify the location of the files relevant to your operating environment. The solutions listed in *The SAS Workbook Solutions* assume that all external raw data files are located in a subdirectory called WORKBOOK on the C: drive of a microcomputer. You may substitute the appropriate file description for the operating environment you are using.

Descriptions of these files, listings of their contents, and a program to create the SAS data set CLINICAL are located in the Appendix.

PROBLEM 1

Reading Raw Data from an External File

Tools

INFILE statement

PAD option (optional)

FILENAME statement (optional)

Data

Raw data file CARS.DTA stored in the subdirectory WORKBOOK on your C: drive

Directions

Write a program that reads this external file and creates a temporary SAS data set called CARS. List the contents of this data set.

PROBLEM 2

Reading More than One Raw Data File to Create a Single SAS Data Set

Tools

INFILE statement

END= option

Data

Two raw data files DEMOG1.DTA and DEMOG2.DTA

Directions

Create a single temporary SAS data set called DEMOG_12 that includes all the data from both of the raw data files.

PROBLEM 3

Reading More than One Raw Data File Using the FILEVAR= Option to Create a Single SAS Data Set

Tools

INFILE statement

FILEVAR= and END= options

Data

The same as Problem 2

Directions

Repeat Problem 2 using the INFILE option FILEVAR= and read the two file names, DEMOG1.DTA and DEMOG2.DTA, from instream data in the DATA step.

CHAPTER 3

**Using Logical Structures:
IF-THEN/ELSE, WHERE, and SELECT**

PROBLEMS

INTRODUCTION

Problems in this chapter require you to use logical statements in the DATA step to create new variables and to group values of an existing variable to create new, recoded variables. Since there are several ways to solve each of these problems, use the Tools list to guide you in selecting appropriate logical statements.

PROBLEM 1

Recoding Age Values Using IF-THEN/ELSE Statements

Tools

IF-THEN/ELSE statements

Data

Raw data file DEMOG1.DTA

Directions

Using the DEMOG1.DTA data file, create a SAS data set called RECODE that includes the subject's age as of January 1, 1996 (rounded to the nearest year) and a variable called AGEGROUP, created with IF-THEN/ELSE statements in the DATA step, with age groups defined as follows:

```
AGEGROUP    Description
-----------------------------------------------
    1       Between 0 and 20 inclusive
    2       Between 21 and 40 inclusive
    3       Between 41 and 60 inclusive
    4       Greater than 60
```

Hint

Use the statement

```
AGE = ROUND (('01JAN96'D - DOB)/365.25);
```

to compute age. This is an approximation and may be incorrect on a person's birthday, depending on whether the current year is a leap year and on how many leap years have occurred between the date of birth and the current date.

PROBLEM 2

Using Logical Statements to Compute a New Data Set Variable

Tools

> IF-THEN/ELSE statements
>> Boolean AND, OR operators

Data

Raw data file CARS.DTA

Directions

A consumer magazine wants to create an index of cars based on the data in the file CARS.DTA. This index is a function of the car size, gas mileage (MILEAGE), and reliability (RELIABLE). The variable SIZE has values SMALL, COMPACT, and MID-SIZED. The rules are as follows:

For SMALL Cars:

Mileage	Reliability	Index
0 to 20	1 to 3	1
0 to 20	4 to 5	2
21 to 50	1 to 3	3
21 to 50	4 to 5	4

For COMPACT Cars:

Mileage	Reliability	Index
0 to 15	1 to 3	1
0 to 15	4 to 5	2
16 to 50	1 to 3	3
16 to 50	4 to 5	4

```
For MID-SIZED Cars:

Mileage          Reliability          Index
---------------------------------------------
  0 to 12          1 to 3              1
  0 to 12          4 to 5              2
 13 to 50          1 to 3              3
 13 to 50          4 to 5              4
```

Write a SAS DATA step to create a SAS data set called CAR_INX that contains all the variables described in the CARS.DTA file plus the INDEX variable. Be sure to set INDEX to a missing value if either a mileage or reliability value is missing.

PROBLEM 3
Using the SELECT Statement to Compute a New Data Set Variable

Tools

SELECT statement

Data

Raw data file CARS.DTA

Directions

Solve Problem 2 using a SELECT statement to test the car size. You may also use it for the other logical tests.

PROBLEM 4
Creating a New Variable Based on Logical Combinations of Existing Data

Tools

IF-THEN/ELSE statements

Boolean AND, OR operators

Data

SAS data set CLINICAL (created by running the program CLINICAL.SAS in the Appendix)

Directions

An organization has created standards of blood pressure for men and women of certain ages. It considers a person to be hypertensive if his or her diastolic blood pressure (DBP) or systolic blood pressure (SBP) is above a critical value. The critical values for DBP and SBP are determined by gender and age range as follows:

```
Gender   Age Range     DBP     SBP
-----------------------------------
 Male     0  - 30       88     152
 Male    31  - 65       92     162
 Male    66 +           94     166
 Female   0  - 30       86     150
 Female  31  - 65       88     158
 Female  66 +           92     164
```

Using the SAS data set CLINICAL and the criteria for hypertension described here, create a new data set called HYPERTEN that contains the variables GENDER, DBP, and SBP from data set CLINICAL, the patient's age at the time of the blood pressure test (drop any fractional part of a year), and a variable HYPER (hypertension) which has values of Y or N depending on the criteria listed above. If either the DBP or SBP is in the hypertensive range, set HYPER = Y (even if the other blood pressure value is missing); if one of the values is missing and the other is in the normal range, assign a missing value to the variable HYPER; if both DBP and SBP are missing, assign a missing value to the variable HYPER.

You can use the SAS statement

```
AGE = INT((VISIT - DOB) / 365.25);
```

to compute the patient's approximate age at the time of his or her blood pressure test.

CHAPTER 4   Combining SAS® Data Sets

PROBLEMS

INTRODUCTION

The information you need for a report or analysis may be contained in more than one raw data file or SAS data set. For example, an employee file may contain some fixed information such as name, social security number, and date of birth. Another file may contain variable information such as the number of sales calls and the dollar amount for each month. A typical report might require you to combine information from these files.

This chapter contains problems related to combining SAS data sets in various ways. The SET, MERGE, and UPDATE statements are all used in this chapter.

PROBLEM 1

Combining Similar Data from Two Different SAS Data Sets

Tools

SET statement

Data

The SAS data set PAY1995 contains payroll data for the year 1995. The variables are ID, LEVEL, SALARY, and GENDER. Data set PAY1996 contains identical information on some new employees. Run the program below to create the two SAS data sets PAY1995 and PAY1996:

```
DATA PAY1995;
   LENGTH ID $ 3 GENDER $ 1;
   INPUT ID LEVEL SALARY GENDER;
DATALINES;
A23 32 68000 M
A24 35 75000 F
A30 44 97000 M
A13 28 27000 F
;
DATA PAY1996;
   LENGTH ID $ 3 GENDER $ 1;
   INPUT ID LEVEL SALARY GENDER;
DATALINES;
A25 29 35000 F
A26 36 88000 F
;
```

Directions

Create a new SAS data set PAY95_96 which contains all the observations from PAY1995 and PAY1996.

PROBLEM 2

Taking a Subset of Observations from a SAS Data Set

Tools

SET statement

Subsetting IF statement or WHERE statement

Data

The SAS data set PAY1995 from Problem 1

Directions

From the observations in the SAS data set PAY1995, create a new data set called FEM_1995, containing information on only female employees.

PROBLEM 3
Creating Multiple SAS Data Sets from a Single SAS Data Set

Tools

> DATA statement (more than one data set name)
> SET, Subsetting IF, and OUTPUT statements

Data

The SAS data set PAY1995 from Problem 1

Directions

From the SAS data set PAY1995, create two SAS data sets, one containing data for females (FEM_1995), the other for males (MAL_1995). Accomplish this in a single DATA step.

PROBLEM 4
Selecting Observations from a SAS Data Set Based on Multiple Conditions

---

Tools

> SET statement
> WHERE statement
> WHERE= data set option
> Date literal ('01JAN70'D)

Data

The SAS data set CLINICAL created by running the program CLINICAL.SAS in the Appendix

Directions

Starting with the SAS data set CLINICAL, create a new data set called OLD_HYP that contains data on all patients born before January 1, 1970 and considered to be hypertensive. For this problem, hypertensive patients are defined as those who have a systolic blood pressure (SBP) greater than 140 or whose diastolic blood pressure (DBP) is greater than 90. Create this data set two ways: using a WHERE statement and using the WHERE= data set option.

PROBLEM 5
Selecting Observations Using Wildcards

Tools

WHERE statement

LIKE operator

Wildcard characters percent sign (%) and underscore (_)

Data

The SAS data set CARS created from the raw data file CARS.DTA

Directions

From the SAS data set CARS, create the following data sets:

A. A data set of all car models which have names beginning with the letter C. Call this data set BEGIN_C.

B. A data set of all car models which have names beginning with the letter C and which have five or fewer characters in the model name. Call this data set BEGIN_C5.

PROBLEM 6
Adding Variables from Two SAS Data Sets Based on an Identifying Variable (Match Merging)

Tools

MERGE statement

PROC SORT

Data

The SAS data set PAY1995 (from Problem 1) and the SAS data set MER1995 created by running the program below:

```
DATA MER1995;
   LENGTH ID $ 3 MERIT $ 1;
   INPUT ID MERIT;
DATALINES;
A28 Y
A23 Y
A24 N
;
```

Directions

Using the SAS data set PAY1995, add merit information, saved in SAS data set MER1995, to each employee. Call the new SAS data set PAYM1995.

Note

There is no merit information for employee A30 in data set MER1995 and the observations are not in ID order.

PROBLEM 7

Adding Summary Information to Each Observation in a SAS Data Set

---

Tools

> MERGE statement
>
> PROC MEANS
>> KEEP= data set option

Data

The SAS data set PAY1995 from Problem 1

Directions

Starting from the SAS data set PAY1995, create a new SAS data set called SAL_PER, containing a new variable, PERCENT. For male employees, PERCENT is computed as the yearly salary (SALARY) expressed as a percentage of the mean salary for all males. For female employees, PERCENT is computed as the yearly salary expressed as a percentage of the mean salary for all females. First, to compute the male and female mean salary and to output this information to a SAS data set (MEAN_SAL), run the program below. The SAS data set MEAN_SAL will contain variables GENDER and M_SALARY.

```
PROC MEANS DATA=PAY1995 NWAY NOPRINT;
   CLASS GENDER;
   VAR SALARY;
   OUTPUT OUT=MEAN_SAL (KEEP=GENDER M_SALARY)
          MEAN=M_SALARY;
RUN;
```

You need to combine the information from MEAN_SAL (two observations) with the information in PAY1995. Then create a new variable (PERCENT) which is 100*SALARY/M_SALARY.

PROBLEM 8
Adding the Information in One SAS Data Set (Containing One Observation) to Every Observation in Another SAS Data Set

Tools
Conditional SET statement
_N_ automatic variable
PROC MEANS

Data
The SAS data set PAY1995 from Problem 1

Directions
Although this problem is similar to Problem 7, the solution is quite different. This time, you compute the mean salary for all employees from the SAS data set PAY1995 and use this number to compute all salaries as a percentage of this mean. Your first step will be to compute the mean salary of all employees (call it GRAND) by running the program below:

```
PROC MEANS DATA=PAY1995 NOPRINT;
   VAR SALARY;
   OUTPUT OUT=MEAN (KEEP=GRAND)
          MEAN=GRAND;
RUN;
```

PROBLEM 9
Updating Values in a SAS Data Set

Tools
PROC SORT
UPDATE statement

Data
The SAS data set PAY1995 from Problem 1

Directions
You have some new values for the employees in data set PAY1995. Employee A23 has a new salary of 72,000; employee A24 is now level 36 with a salary of 77,000; employee A13 was mistakenly entered as a female (F) instead of male (M). Create a SAS data set with this new information and update data set PAY1995, creating a new SAS data set PAY1995C (C for "corrected") which reflects the updated information.

PROBLEM 10
Combining Variables from Two SAS Data Sets

Tools

MERGE statement
   IN= and KEEP= data set options

Data

The SAS data set PAY1995 from Problem 1 and a SAS data set called BALL, created by running
the program below

```
DATA BALL;
    LENGTH ID $ 3.;
    INPUT ID HEIGHT;
DATALINES;
A24 65
A13 66
A23 72
;
```

Directions

Some of the employees in data set PAY1995 (the original, not the updated one) want to form
a basketball team (albeit, a small one). A SAS data set called BALL contains the ID and height
(in inches) of these individuals. Create a new SAS data set, TEAM, which includes the employee
number (ID), GENDER, and HEIGHT. Include only those employees who are in data set BALL.

PROBLEM 11
Merging SAS Data Sets with Multiple BY Variables

Tools

MERGE statement

Data

Medical allowance data for each gender and level as follows

Gender	Level	Allowance
F	28	2,000
M	28	1,800
F	32	2,100
M	32	1,900
F	35	2,200
M	35	2,000
F	44	4,000
M	44	3,600

Directions

For each value of GENDER and LEVEL for employees in the PAY1995 data set, you have an allowance limit as shown in the Data section. Create a SAS data set with this information. Then create a new SAS data set called PAY1995H which contains the original variables from PAY1995 plus the health allowance information. This new data set should not contain health allowance information for any combinations of GENDER and LEVEL that are not represented in data set PAY1995.

Hint

Read in the allowance values using a COMMA5. informat.

PROBLEM 12
Merging Data from Multiple SAS Data Sets and Selecting Observations

Tools

> MERGE statement
> > IN= data set option
> Subsetting IF statement

Data

The SAS data set CLINICAL, plus the two SAS data sets TREAD and FAT which can be created by running the following SAS program

```
DATA TREAD;
    INPUT ID     $ 1-3
          MINUTES 4-5;
DATALINES;
123 10
811 12
586 14
278 11
193 12
;
DATA FAT;
    INPUT ID       $ 1-3
          BODY_FAT   5-6;
DATALINES;
444 14
123 23
919 18
278 20
444 24
811 34
193 30
;
```

Directions

Some of the patients from the SAS data set CLINICAL entered two studies. In one study, the length of time on a treadmill (MINUTES) was measured and stored in data set TREAD. In the other study, the subject's percent of body fat (BODY_FAT) was measured and stored in data set FAT. Combine all the information from data sets CLINICAL, TREAD, and FAT and create a new SAS data set called STUDY. Keep only those subjects who have both the treadmill data and the percent body fat measured.

PROBLEM 13

Using the MERGE Statement to Perform a Table Lookup

Tools

MERGE statement
BY statement, with multiple BY variables

Data

SAS data set CLINICAL and blood pressure limits as described in Chapter 3, Problem 4

Directions

Solve Problem 4 in Chapter 3 by first creating a SAS data set of upper limits for systolic and diastolic blood pressure by age group and gender. Then merge this data set with a new SAS data set created from CLINICAL that contains a variable called AGEGROUP corresponding to the age groupings in Chapter 3, Problem 4, along with GENDER, DBP, and SBP. Use this new merged data set to create the variable HYPER with values of Y or N as defined.

CHAPTER 5   Using Numerical Functions

PROBLEMS

INTRODUCTION

Problems in this chapter involve many of the SAS numerical functions. Chapter 6 is devoted to character functions. Even if you don't normally use mathematical functions such as LOG or SIN, there are many other numerical functions that have uses such as counting the number of missing or non-missing values in a list of variables or obtaining values of variables from previous observations. Here are some problems that demonstrate some of the SAS numerical functions.

PROBLEM 1

Using Numerical Functions to Create New Variables

Tools

ROUND, LOG, LOG10, INT, MIN, MAX, MEAN, SUM, and N functions

Data

Raw data values for variables X, Y, and Z

```
X        Y        Z
------------------
1        2        3
4        .        6
2.33     5        .
2.5      2.6      2.7
```

Directions

Given the data for variables X, Y, and Z, write a SAS DATA step to create a SAS data set called XYZ which contains the following new variables:

```
New Variable        Description
------------------------------------------------------------
ROUND_X       X rounded to the nearest tenth
LOG_X         The base e log of X
LOG_10X       The base 10 log of X
WHOLE_X       The integer part of X
SMALL         The smallest value of X, Y, or Z
BIG           The largest value of X, Y, or Z
AVE           The mean of the non-missing values of X, Y, and Z
SUM           The sum of the non-missing values of X, Y, and Z
NONMISS       The number of non-missing values of X, Y, and Z
```

PROBLEM 2

Choosing Every Third Observation

Tools

MOD function

_N_ automatic variable

Data

SAS data set WHOLE created by running the following program

```
DATA WHOLE;
   DO SUBJECT = 1 TO 12;
      ***Generate uniform random numbers from 1 to 100;
      SCORE = INT(100 * RANUNI(0) + 1);
      OUTPUT;
   END;
RUN;
```

Directions

Use the automatic variable _N_ (sometimes thought of as an observation counter but more accurately it actually counts iterations of the DATA step) along with the MOD function to read every third observation from an existing SAS data set WHOLE, starting with the first observation. The new data set will contain the first, fourth, seventh, and so on, observation from data set WHOLE.

PROBLEM 3
Computing a Moving Average

Tools
LAG and LAG*n* functions

_N_ automatic variable

Data
Month and cost figures as shown

```
MONTH      COST
---------------
 JAN       125
 FEB       120
 MAR       130
 APR       100
 MAY       140
 JUN       180
 JUL       200
```

Directions
Compute a moving average of COST using the value for the current month and the value from the two previous months. For example, the moving average of COST for March would be the mean of COST for January, February, and March. For the first two months where you don't have two previous months of data, set the moving average to missing.

Hint
The moving average for JAN and FEB should be missing. For MAR it should be the mean of 125, 120, and 130. For APR it should be the mean of 120, 130, and 100, and so on.

PROBLEM 4
Computing Averages within an Observation

Tools
N and MEAN functions

Data

Sample survey data as follows

```
ID   QUES1 QUES2 QUES3 QUES4 QUES5 QUES6 QUES7 QUES8 QUES9 QUES10
--------------------------------------------------------------------
 1     3     4     3     2     .     5     5     4     4     3
 2     .     .     .     2     1     1     1     2     1     2
 3     5     4     5     3     3     4     5     4     .     5
```

Directions

A survey asking questions about the environment was administered to some children. Compute an overall score by taking the mean of the ten questions. However, the overall score should only be computed if eight or more of the ten questions are answered. Write a SAS DATA step to compute this overall score.

PROBLEM 5

Computing Differences between Observations

Tools

DIF and DIF*n* functions

Data

SAS data set WHOLE from Problem 2

Directions

Using the SAS data set WHOLE, write a program that will compute

A. The difference between the value of SCORE for the present subject and the value of SCORE for the previous subject. (The difference is missing for SUBJECT=1.)

B. The difference between the value of SCORE for the present subject and the value of SCORE for a subject two observations prior. For example, the first non-missing difference will be the value of SCORE for subject three minus the value of SCORE for subject one.

PROBLEM 6

Computing Differences and Sums among Observations

Tools

LAG, LAG*n*, DIF, DIF*n*, and MEAN functions

SET and BY statements

LAST.*variable* temporary variable

Data

SAS data set MULTIPLE created by running the following SAS program

```
DATA MULTIPLE;
    INPUT SUBJECT 1-2 X 4 Y 6 Z 8;
DATALINES;
01 1 2 3
01 4 5 6
01 7 8 9
02 8 7 6
02 5 4 3
02 2 1 0
;
```

Directions

Using data set MULTIPLE which has three observations per subject, create a new data set called ONE which has one observation per subject and contains the following

A. The difference between the third value of X, Y, and Z and the second value for each subject.

B. The difference between the third value of X, Y, and Z and the first value for each subject.

C. The mean of X, Y, and Z for each subject.

Note

Do not use PROC MEANS to solve part C.

PROBLEM 7

Performing Character to Numeric Conversion

Tools

INPUT function

RENAME= data set option (if you take the challenge)

Data

SAS data set CHAR created by running the following program

```
DATA CHAR;
    INPUT AGE $ HEIGHT $ WEIGHT $;
DATALINES;
23 68 160
44 72 200
55  . 180
;
```

Directions

Given the data set CHAR, convert AGE, HEIGHT, and WEIGHT to numeric values. If you would like a bit more of a challenge, give the numeric variables in the new data set the same name as the original names in data set CHAR.

PROBLEM 8

Performing Some Simple Trigonometric Computations

Tools

SIN, COS, TAN, ARSIN, ARCOS, and ATAN functions

Data

Various trigonometric values as follows

DEGREE	RADIAN	SINE	COSINE	TANGENT
30	1	.5	.5	.5
45	3.14159	1	1	1
0	.5708	.707	.707	0
390	10	.003	.003	.003

Directions

You want to read in some raw data representing angles (some in degrees, others in radians) and some trigonometric values for which you want to compute angles (both in degrees and radians).

Compute the sine, cosine, and tangent of DEGREE and RADIAN, and find the angles in degrees and radians corresponding to the SINE, COSINE, and TANGENT values. That is, find the arcsine of SINE, the arccosine of COSINE, and the arctangent of TANGENT, and express these angles in degrees and radians.

PROBLEM 9
Dropping the Lowest Grade

Tools

N and MEAN functions

ARRAY statement (optional)

Data

Student quiz grades as follows

STUDENT	QUIZ1	QUIZ2	QUIZ3	QUIZ4	QUIZ5
Baggett	4	2	6	2	3
Ginn	9	9	10	.	9
Cody	10	10	9	10	10
Smith	.	.	2	3	4

Directions

Being the nice teacher that you are, you decide to drop the lowest of five quiz grades if a student took all five quizzes. Write a program that will compute the mean quiz grade based on this decision. If the student took fewer than five quizzes, compute the mean of the non-missing quizzes.

CHAPTER 6 — Using Character Functions

INTRODUCTION

SAS software provides a powerful assortment of character functions that allow you to perform a variety of useful string operations. Because of the large number and flexibility of these functions, there are usually several solutions to the problems presented here. No single solution is *the* correct solution. You may want to take a hint from the functions listed in the Tools list but feel free to find other innovative solutions as well. To accommodate alternative solutions, the Tools list may also include more functions than you need.

PROBLEM 1

Reading a Mixture of Numbers and Letters from Raw Data

Tools

LENGTH, SUBSTR, INPUT, INDEX, and COMPRESS functions

LENGTH statement

Double trailing at sign (@@)

Data

A single line of temperature values

```
32F   42C   137F   84F   20C
```

Directions

Temperatures in degrees Celsius and degrees Fahrenheit are mixed together in an input data stream. Celsius temperatures appear in the form *nnn*C, where *nnn* is a 1 to 3 digit number.

Fahrenheit temperatures are entered as *nnn*F. Write a program to read the sample data and store all temperatures in degrees Celsius. The conversion from Fahrenheit to Celsius is

C = (F - 32)*5/9   where C = temperature in degrees Celsius and

F = temperature in degrees Fahrenheit

PROBLEM 2
Checking for Invalid Data Values

Tools
VERIFY function

Data
IDs and multiple choice (A - E) responses

```
001ABCDEABCDE
002XCCBEBBABC
003A BACECBAA
004abcdeabcde
```

A student ID is stored in columns 1-3, and the item responses are stored in columns 4-13.

Directions
Answers to a ten-item multiple choice test are entered in a file. Valid responses are A, B, C, D, or E (upper case only) and blank. Write a program that will write the student ID and the invalid data to a SAS data set called INVALID for any student having one or more invalid data values for the ten items. You may place the data lines in a data file and have your program read it or you may place these data lines "instream," following a DATALINES statement, to test your program.

Hint
You can read all ten items into a single ten-byte character string.

Note
The data set INVALID should contain the observations for ID numbers 002 (the X for item 1) and 004 (all lowercase responses).

PROBLEM 3
"Unpacking" a Character String

Tools
SUBSTR and INPUT functions
ARRAY statement (optional)

Data

SAS data set PACK created by running the following program

```
DATA PACK;
   INPUT TEN $10.;
DATALINES;
0123456789
1 2 3 4 56
3428645889
;
```

Directions

You are given a SAS data set PACK that contains a ten-byte character variable (TEN) where each byte is a numeral 0 to 9 or a blank (representing a missing value). Write a program that will read this data set and create a new data set called UNPACK that contains ten numeric variables (X1-X10) from the ten-byte character variable.

PROBLEM 4

Substituting One Character for Another in a String

Tools

TRANSLATE function

ARRAY statement (optional)

Data

Five responses to a multiple choice test

```
12345
3 414
54321
```

Directions

Data values for five multiple choice questions were entered as digits 1-5 (or blank) rather than the letters A-E. Write a program that will read the digits (you may read them as character values), convert them to the corresponding letters, and create a SAS data set called CONVERT that contains five character variables. For example, 1 would be converted to A, 2 to B, and so on.

PROBLEM 5
Cleaning Data and Substituting Characters

Tools

UPCASE, TRANSLATE, and VERIFY functions (suggested possibilities)

ARRAY statement (optional)

Data

Five responses to a multiple choice test

```
12345
aBcDe
xY73E
3 E w
```

Directions

This problem is similar to the previous one except that prior to the substitution of A for 1, B for 2, and so on, you have to do some data cleaning. As in Problem 4, you have five responses to test questions in columns 1 through 5, and you want to create five variables QUES1- QUES5. The raw data consist of some numerals, some data already entered as A-E, some data errors (numerals above 5 and letters other than A-E), and a mixture of upper- and lowercase. Convert all letters to uppercase and substitute the letters A through E for the numerals 1 through 5. Convert any remaining data values (letters other than A-E or numerals not in the range of 1 to 5) to a character missing value. You may want to use an array to make this program more compact.

PROBLEM 6
Creating a Simple Substitution Cipher

Tools

TRANSLATE and UPCASE functions

FILE and PUT statements (optional)

DATA _NULL_ (optional)

Data

Lines of "plain text" as follows

```
This is TEST
Line TWO of the Message
```

Directions

This problem and the one that follows deal with a simple substitution cipher. You may have some fun giving a cipher to a friend and seeing if he or she can decipher it by using letter frequencies.

Now for the problem. You want to encode plain text into a simple substitution cipher. That is, you want to substitute one letter for another to create a simple coded message. Have your program read lines of plain text (in upper- or lowercase) and write the encoded message (all in uppercase) to a print file (or to the LOG).

The correspondence key is as follows

```
A=Q B=W C=E D=R E=T F=Y G=U H=I I=O J=P K=L L=K M=J
N=H O=G P=F Q=D R=S S=A T=Z U=X V=C W=V X=B Y=N Z=M
```

Use the two lines of data in the Data section to test your program.
The output should look as follows

```
ZIOA OA Q ZTAZ
KOHT ZVG GY ZIT JTAAQUT
```

PROBLEM 7
Deciphering a Simple Substitution Cipher

Tools

> TRANSLATE function
>
> FILE and PUT statements (optional)
>
> DATA _NULL_ (optional)

Data

The encoded message from Problem 6

```
ZIOA OA Q ZTAZ
KOHT ZVG GY ZIT JTAAQUT
```

Directions

This problem is the reverse of Problem 6. Here, you want a program that will read the encoded message and turn it back into plain text. Use the reverse letter substitutions to do this. For example, Q=A, W=B, and so on.

CHAPTER 7 | Working with Dates

PROBLEMS

INTRODUCTION

Date values represent an interesting challenge in most programming languages. SAS software has an extensive set of tools for working with dates. This section allows you to practice with some of these tools.

PROBLEM 1

Reading Dates in a Variety of Configurations

Tools

Date informats and formats

Data

Date values in a variety of styles

```
          1         2         3         4
12345678901234567890123456789012345678901234 5
---------------------------------------------
102146 10/21/46 21OCT46 46294 211046 10211946
122596 12/25/96 25DEC96 96360 251296 12251996
```

Directions

You are given raw data which contains dates in a variety of styles (MM/DD/YY, Julian, and so on) as in the Data section. Write a program to read these dates and create a SAS data set called IN_DATE. List the contents of IN_DATE, printing all the dates in MM/DD/YY format. The date formats are

```
Variable        Starting Column     Date Format
----------------------------------------------
  DATE1              1               MMDDYY
  DATE2              8               MM/DD/YY
  DATE3             17               DDMONYY
  DATE4             25               YYNNN (Julian)
  DATE5             31               DDMMYY
  DATE6             38               MMDDYYYY
```

PROBLEM 2
Reading Dates in Non-standard Forms

Tools

MDY and ROUND functions

Data

Month, day, and year data scattered about

```
           1         2         3         4
123456789012345678901234567890123456789012345
----------------------------------------------
   17    09    1990 04 96
   30    11    1991 05 95
```

Directions

You inherited some interesting data which has date information (month, day, and year) scattered about in different locations. In addition, one of the date values only has year and month (day is missing), and you want to create a SAS date using the 15th of the month in place of the missing day. The information to create the first date (DATE1) is

```
Day       columns 3-4
Month     columns 10-11
Year      columns 15-18
```

For the second date (DATE2)

```
Day is missing
Month     columns 20-21
Year      columns 23-24
```

Using the sample data, create a SAS data set called IN_DATE2, containing the variables DATE1 and DATE2 as SAS date values, and compute the number of years (rounded to the nearest year) between DATE1 and DATE2. Print out the contents of IN_DATE2 using the format WORDDATE*w.* for the variables DATE1 and DATE2.

PROBLEM 3
Computing Approximate Age in Years

Tools
INT, ROUND, and TODAY functions

KEEP statement or KEEP= data set option

Date literal

Data
SAS data set CLINICAL

Directions
Using the SAS data set CLINICAL, create a new SAS data set called AGE that contains the variables AGE1-AGE3, where these variables are the person's approximate age in years computed as follows:

AGE1	Age as of 1/1/96 rounded to the nearest year
AGE2	Age at the time of the VISIT, with any fractional part of a year dropped (e.g. 25.9 years would be changed to 25 years)
AGE3	Age, rounded to the nearest half year, as of the date the program is run (i.e. today's date).

Include in this new data set the variables ID, DOB, and VISIT (from CLINICAL) and the three computed variables AGE1-AGE3. Note that there is a data error in data set CLINICAL (put there on purpose for a later problem) where the VISIT date is earlier than the date of birth. Just ignore this when doing this problem.

PROBLEM 4
Computing the Day of the Week, Month of the Year, and Year for a Given Date

Tools
WEEKDAY, MONTH, and YEAR functions

KEEP statement or KEEP= data set option

PROC FORMAT

PROC FREQ

Data
SAS data set CLINICAL

Directions

Using the variable VISIT (date of visit) from the data set CLINICAL, create a new data set (CLINDATE) containing the variables ID and VISIT from CLINICAL plus three new variables, DAY_WEEK, MONTH, and YEAR which represent the day of the week, month of the year, and year, respectively. Create formats for DAY_WEEK and MONTH. Count frequencies for DAY_WEEK, MONTH, and YEAR.

Note

The solution shown uses an option to omit the cumulative frequencies. You may choose to do this or not.

PROBLEM 5
Creating Day of the Week and Month of the Year Variables without Using a User-created Format

Tools

    PUT function

    WEEKDATE*w.* and MONNAME*w.* formats

Data

Same as Problem 4

Directions

This problem is similar to the previous one except you want the values for DAY_WEEK to be character values of MON, TUE, WED, and so on, and values of MONTH to be JAN, FEB, and so on, without using any user-defined formats. Compute frequencies for DAY_WEEK and MONTH.

CHAPTER 8 | Using Arrays

PROBLEMS

INTRODUCTION

Use explicit arrays to solve all the problems in this chapter. Although the older implicit arrays can be used to solve some of the problems, the newer implicit form of the ARRAY statement is preferred and is used in all the solutions. If you are having trouble solving a problem, try writing out a few lines of code without using an array. Then create your array containing the variables in the repeated lines. Finally, using one of the sample lines as a template, substitute the array name for the variable name and, if necessary, place the statement in a DO loop.

PROBLEM 1

Using an Array to Set Values of 9, 99, and 999 to Missing for a Series of Numeric Variables

Tools

ARRAY statement (numeric variables)

Data

SAS data set LOTS_9 created by running the following program

```
DATA LOTS_9;
   INPUT X1-X5 A B C D Y1-Y5 Z1-Z3;
DATALINES;
1 0 1 0 1 2 2 2 1 2 3 4 5 3 3 3
9 0 0 0 9 99 99 99 7 999 999 4 5 6 999 999 999
;
```

Directions

You have a SAS data set called LOTS_9 where values of 9, 99, and 999 are to be converted to missing values as follows

```
Variables          Value to be Converted to Missing
-----------------------------------------------------
X1-X5                      9
A,B,C,D                   99
Y1-Y5, Z1-Z3             999
```

Create a new data set LOTSMISS, replacing the appropriate values of 9, 99, and 999 with a SAS missing value. Be sure to convert only the appropriate values 9, 99, or 999 to missing for the variables in question. For example, a value of 9 is NOT a missing value for variables A, B, C, D, Y1- Y5, or Z1-Z3.

PROBLEM 2

Converting a Value of "NA" to Missing for Character Variables

Tools

ARRAY statement (character variables)
UPCASE and DIM functions (optional)

Data

SAS data set NOTAPPLY created by running the following program

```
DATA NOTAPPLY;
   LENGTH A B C D E $ 2;
   INPUT ID A $ B $ C $ D $ E $ X Y Z;
DATALINES;
001 Y N N Y Y 1 2 3
002 na NA Y Y Y 3 4 5
003 NA NA NA na na 8 9 10
;
```

Directions

In the SAS data set NOTAPPLY, a value of either NA or na was used in place of a missing value for all character variables. Create a new SAS data set NEW where these values are converted to a character missing value.

Hint

Be careful to test for both upper- and lowercase values of NA. You may want to have two tests or use the UPCASE function.

PROBLEM 3
Converting Fahrenheit Temperatures to Celsius for Lots of Variables

Tools

ARRAY statement

Data

SAS data set TEMPER created by running the following program

```
DATA TEMPER;
   ARRAY F[30]; *** Equivalent to ARRAY F[30] F1-F30;

   DO OBS = 1 TO 5;
      DO I = 1 TO 30;
         ***The line below will randomly generate temperatures
            from 32 to 212;
         F[I] = INT(RANUNI(0)*181 + 32);
      END;
      OUTPUT;
   END;

   KEEP F1-F30;
RUN;
```

Directions

A SAS data set called TEMPER contains variables F1-F30 which represent 30 temperatures in degrees Fahrenheit. Create a new data set called TEMPER2 that contains only the variables C1-C30 which are these temperatures converted to degrees Celsius. The Fahrenheit to Celsius conversion is

Degrees Celsius = 5/9 x (Degrees Fahrenheit - 32)

PROBLEM 4

Creating Several Observations from a Single Observation

Tools

ARRAY and OUTPUT statements

Data

SAS data set DIAG created by running the following program

```
DATA DIAG;
    INFILE DATALINES PAD;
    INPUT @1  ID  $3.
          @5 (DX1-DX5)($2. + 1);
DATALINES;
001 11 12
002 01 02 03 04 05
003 12
004 05 06
005 AA BB CC DD EE
;
```

Directions

The data set DIAG contains a patient ID and up to five diagnosis codes (DX1-DX5) per observation. To help you visualize the data set, here is a listing of its contents.

```
        Listing of Data Set DIAG
```

Patient ID	DX1	DX2	DX3	DX4	DX5
001	11	12			
002	01	02	03	04	05
003	12				
004	05	06			
005	AA	BB	CC	DD	EE

Using arrays, create a new data set called DIAG2 that contains up to five observations per patient. Each observation should contain the patient ID and a single variable (DX) which is also a two-byte character variable and is equal to DX1, DX2, and so on, for each of the one to five possible observations per patient in DIAG2. Do not output an observation in DIAG2 if a diagnosis is missing. For example, the first seven observations in data set DIAG2 should look like this

```
ID    DX
--------
001   11
001   12
002   01
002   02
002   03
002   04
002   05
```

PROBLEM 5
Creating One Observation from Several Observations

Tools

ARRAY and RETAIN statements

FIRST.*variable* and LAST.*variable* temporary variables

Data

SAS data set MANY created by running the following program

```
DATA MANY;
      INPUT ID TIME X Y Z;
      DATALINES;
      1    1    1    2    3
      1    2    4    5    6
      1    3    7    8    9
      2    1    10   20   30
      2    3    40   .    50
      3    1    15   .    .
      3    2    25   26   27
      3    3    35   36   37
      ;
```

Directions

Write a program to restructure the data set MANY, which contains from one to three observations per ID, to a new data set ONEPER, which contains only one observation per ID. To help you visualize data set MANY, here is a listing of its contents

```
ID    TIME    X     Y     Z
 1     1      1     2     3
 1     2      4     5     6
 1     3      7     8     9
 2     1      10    20    30     Note: TIME = 2 is missing for
 2     3      40    .     50           ID = 2
 3     1      15    .     .
 3     2      25    26    27
 3     3      35    36    37
```

The variables in the new data set ONEPER are ID, X1-X3, Y1-Y3, and Z1-Z3. They represent the values of X, Y, and Z at times 1, 2, and 3, respectively. Data set ONEPER should look like this

```
ID  X1   X2   X3   Y1   Y2   Y3   Z1   Z2   Z3
 1   1    4    7    2    5    8    3    6    9
 2  10    .   40   20    .    .   30    .   15
 3  15   25   35    .   26   36    .   27   37
```

Note

Check your ONEPER data set to be sure that you have missing values for X2, Y2, and Z2 for ID = 2.

PROBLEM 6
Choosing Upper and Lower Bounds for an Array

Tools

ARRAY statement (upper and lower boundary specified)

Data

SAS data set PAYROLL created by running the following program

```
DATA PAYROLL;
    INPUT AMT1990-AMT1996;
DATALINES;
50000 55000 57000 62000 66000 70000 72000
40000 43000 44000 55000 65000 69000 73000
;
```

Directions

A SAS data set called PAYROLL contains the variables AMT1990 through AMT1996. Using an array with lower and upper bounds equal to 1990 and 1996 respectively, write a SAS DATA step to create a new data set called TAXES that contains the original AMT variables plus the variables TAX1990 through TAX1996. Each TAX variable is obtained by multiplying the corresponding AMT variable by .25.

PROBLEM 7
Using a Temporary Array to Hold Passing Scores on a Test

Tools

Temporary array

Data

Student names and test scores as shown

STUDENT	TEST1	TEST2	TEST3	TEST4	TEST5
Bob	45	68	80	65	60
Michelle	80	90	95	90	87
Clifton	59	69	79	89	99

Directions

The passing scores on five tests are 65, 70, 65, 70, and 75. Using a temporary array to hold the passing scores, count the number of tests passed by each of the students.

CHAPTER 9	Looking Back and Ahead Across Observations

PROBLEMS

INTRODUCTION

This chapter contains problems that require you to either look back or look ahead across observations. This is especially important when you have more than one observation per subject in a data set. You may want to compare a value in the present observation to a value from a previous observation for the same subject.

Looking back usually requires such tools as the RETAIN statement, the LAG function, FIRST.*variable* and LAST.*variable*. Sometimes, you can look back by restructuring the data set so that what was originally multiple observations is now contained in a single observation. Looking ahead is more difficult and is most easily accomplished by using more than one SET statement with the FIRSTOBS= data set option set to different values.

PROBLEM 1

"Copying" Values from One Observation to Another Observation

Tools

RETAIN statement

FIRST.*variable* and LAST.*variable* temporary variables (possibly)

Data

Raw data file DIALYSIS.DTA

Directions

You have a longitudinal data file of visits to a dialysis center called DIALYSIS.DTA. The first record for each patient includes an ID, a visit number (VISIT), a date of birth (DOB), GENDER, heart rate (HR), systolic blood pressure (SBP), and diastolic blood pressure (DBP). Subsequent records for the same patient only contain data for the ID, VISIT, HR, SBP, and DBP. That is, the DOB and GENDER information is only entered on the first record for each patient. There are a variable number of visits for each patient.

Create a data set containing the values for DOB and GENDER included in every observation. You may assume that there are no missing IDs. The DOB and GENDER may be missing for all visits for some patients. Solve this problem using a RETAIN statement to "remember" the DOB and GENDER. You may want to try this "on the fly" by reading the raw data (file DIALYSIS.DTA) directly or you may choose to create a SAS data set first and then process this in a subsequent DATA step.

PROBLEM 2
Computing a Moving Average

Tools

LAG function

_N_ automatic variable

Data

Daily stock prices as follows

DATE	PRICE
01/01/95	23.00
01/02/95	25.00
01/03/95	24.00
01/04/95	29.00
01/05/95	26.00
01/06/95	23.00
01/07/95	24.00

Directions

You have a raw data file which contains the date and the closing price for a particular stock. You want to compute a moving average which is the mean of today's price and the price for the previous two days. Create a data set that contains the date, the current price, and the moving average, starting with day three. Provide a listing of the data set (use an appropriate format for the dollar amounts). Plot the daily price and the three-day moving average versus the date on one set of axes, using a separate plotting symbol for each of the two plots.

Note

Problem 3 in Chapter 5 is similar to this problem and also involves computing a moving average.

PROBLEM 3
Looking Back

Tools

LAG function

Data

Raw data consisting of three records per subject as follows

```
ID    TRIAL    X    Y    Z
-------------------------
1      1       1    2    3
1      2       2    3    6
1      3       4    1    2
2      1       4    5    6
9      2       5    4    3
2      3       1    2    1
3      1       2    2    2
3      2       3    3    3
3      3       4    5    6
```

Directions

You conducted an experiment where each subject underwent three trials. For each trial, an ID number, a trial number (NUMBER), and three variables (X, Y, and Z) were measured. Each subject has exactly three records. Write a program that checks if the IDs are the same in all three records. If they are, write out the observations to data set OK; if not, write out the three observations to data set NOT_OK.

Hint

The first three and the last three records should end up in data set OK; the middle three records should end up in data set NOT_OK.

PROBLEM 4
Looking Ahead

Tools

SET statement

FIRSTOBS=, RENAME=, and DROP= data set options

Data

SAS data set STREP created by running the following program

```
DATA STREP;
   INFILE DATALINES PAD;
   INPUT @1  ID      $1
         @3  VISIT   MMDDYY8.
         @12 DOCTOR  $3.;
DATALINES;
1 11/01/95 ABC
1 12/01/95 XYZ
2 12/01/95 JBD
2 12/07/95 RPC
3 01/05/96 ABC
3 05/05/96 JBD
3 07/01/96 XYZ

;
```

Directions

You have a SAS data set called STREP which has information on patients visiting a clinic who have a diagnosis of strep throat. Each observation contains a patient ID, visit date (VISIT), and DOCTOR initials. If the same patient returns for a visit within 90 days for strep throat, a variable called OUTCOME is to be set to the value FAILURE. If the patient returns more than 90 days later or has no further visits, the variable OUTCOME is to be set to a value of SUCCESS. You may assume that there are no missing values for visit date or doctor initials.

You want to assign the responsibility (blame?) for this success or failure to the doctor who originally saw the patient. You could "remember" the previous value of DOCTOR with a retained variable or use a LAG function. However, for this problem, you are to look ahead (see the Tools list for a hint) to see if the next visit is within 90 days and if it is the same patient. Write a SAS program that looks ahead to the next observation, creates a new data set called BLAME, and sets the value of OUTCOME for the visit where the patient is seen by the doctor who will be assigned the responsibility.

The data set BLAME should have seven observations as shown below

OBS	ID	VISIT	DOCTOR	OUTCOME
1	1	11/01/95	ABC	FAILURE
2	1	12/01/95	XYZ	SUCCESS
3	2	12/01/95	JBD	FAILURE
4	2	12/07/95	RPC	SUCCESS
5	3	01/05/96	ABC	SUCCESS
6	3	05/05/96	JBD	FAILURE
7	3	07/01/96	XYZ	SUCCESS

Hint

The blank record at the end of the raw data will make your program a bit easier to write.

| **CHAPTER 10** | **Working with Longitudinal Data: Multiple Observations per Subject** |

PROBLEMS

INTRODUCTION

Problems in this chapter deal with the special challenges associated with longitudinal data, that is, data with multiple observations per subject. Many of the same tools you used in the last chapter will be used here. In addition some of the projects in Chapter 21 require the techniques used here.

PROBLEM 1

Selecting the First or Last Observation per Subject

Tools

FIRST.*variable* and LAST.*variable* temporary variables

Data

Raw data file CLIN_X.DTA

Directions

Create two data sets from the CLIN_X.DTA raw data file. The first data set (call it FIRST) should consist of the first visit for each patient. The other data set (call it LAST) should contain the last visit for each patient. If any patient has only one visit, include this visit in both data sets. Try to create both data sets in a single DATA step.

Hint

Be careful. The raw data file is not in order by ID or by date of visit.

PROBLEM 2

Selecting All Patients with N Observations (DATA Step Approach)

Tools

FIRST.*variable* and LAST.*variable* temporary variables

SUM and MERGE statements

IN= data set option

WHERE or IF statement or WHERE= data set option

Data

Raw data file CLIN_X.DTA

Directions

Create a data set of all patients in the CLIN_X.DTA data file that have exactly four visits. For this problem, accomplish the task by first counting the number of visits for each patient using a DATA step. Create a data set containing data on only those patients with four visits. This data set should have one observation per patient and a single variable (ID). Combine this information with a data set created from the original data to produce the final data set. The resulting data set should contain four observations for each of two patients.

PROBLEM 3

Selecting All Patients with N Observations (Using a Procedure to Do Some of the Work)

Tools

PROC MEANS or PROC FREQ

MERGE statement

IN= data set option

WHERE or IF statement or WHERE= data set option

Data

Raw data file CLIN_X.DTA

Directions

This problem is the same as Problem 2, except that you should first use PROC MEANS or PROC FREQ to create a data set containing all patients with exactly four visits. From that point, proceed as you did before.

Hint

If you choose to use PROC MEANS, pick any numeric variable and use the _FREQ_ variable (the number of observations, missing or non-missing) to count the number of visits per patient.

PROBLEM 4

Copying Data from the First Record to Replace Missing Values on Subsequent Records (Method 1)

Tools

    RETAIN statement
    FIRST.*variable* temporary variable

Data

Raw data file BASKETBA.DTA (see the Appendix)

Directions

You are given the data file BASKETBA.DTA. Notice that values for ID, GENDER, HEIGHT, and DATE are entered only on the first record for each player while the number of points scored is entered on every record. Create a SAS data set called BASKET that has values for ID, GENDER, HEIGHT, DATE, and POINTS for every observation. For this problem, use the FIRST.*variable* temporary variable and a RETAIN statement to accomplish the task.

Note

A. This problem is similar to Problem 1 from Chapter 9.

B. It might have been smarter to have two data sets, one containing ID, GENDER, and HEIGHT (demographic data) and another containing ID, DATE, and POINTS. However, the data set was constructed this way to give you some programming practice.

Hint

Be especially careful since GENDER and HEIGHT are missing for a few players.

PROBLEM 5

Copying Data from the First Record to Replace Missing Values on Subsequent Records (Method 2)

Tools

FIRST.*variable* temporary variable

DROP= and KEEP= data set options

MERGE statement

Data

Raw data file BASKETBA.DTA

Directions

Solve Problem 4, except create one data set containing the first observation for each player with the variables ID, GENDER, and HEIGHT. Merge this with the original data set (dropping GENDER and HEIGHT), thus adding the missing information to the other observations.

PROBLEM 6

Computing Differences Across Observations

Tools

FIRST.*variable* and LAST.*variable* temporary variables

RETAIN statement

Data

Raw data file CLIN_X.DTA

Directions

Create a SAS data set from the CLIN_X.DTA data file. Compute the difference between the heart rate, the systolic blood pressure, and the diastolic blood pressure from the first visit to the last visit for all patients who had two or more visits (that is, the value at the last visit minus the value at the first visit).

PROBLEM 7
Counting Code Values in a DATA Step

Tools

ARRAY (optional) and RETAIN statements

PROC SORT

FIRST.*variable* and LAST.*variable* temporary variables

Data

SAS data set DRUG created by running the following program

```
DATA DRUG;
    INPUT ID DATE : MMDDYY8. RX1-RX3;
    FORMAT DATE MMDDYY8.;
DATALINES;
1 10/21/95 1 0 0
1 10/22/95 2 0 1
1 10/23/95 0 0 1
2 09/02/95 1 1 1
2 09/03/95 1 1 1
3 11/11/95 0 2 1
3 11/15/95 0 0 2
;
```

Directions

Each time a patient comes in for a clinic visit, information is recorded on each of three drugs. A code of 0 indicates the drug is not being taken; a code of 1 indicates the drug is being started; a code of 2 indicates that the drug is being discontinued. For each visit, a patient ID, visit date (DATE), and status on each of the three drugs (RX1-RX3) is recorded. Write a SAS program that will count the number of patients who were ever on each of the three drugs (a code of 1 or 2 on any visit). Try using only DATA step operations (plus PROC SORT). Use a PUT statement to write the number of patients on the three drugs to a print or log file.

CHAPTER 11

Writing Simple DATA Step Reports

PROBLEMS

INTRODUCTION

This chapter contains some basic DATA step reporting problems. PROC PRINT and PROC REPORT can be used to create a variety of reports, but sometimes you require more flexibility, and you need to resort to the keyword DATA _NULL_ and PUT statements to get the job done. Here are some reporting problems where you are asked to use the DATA step to solve the problem.

PROBLEM 1

Writing a Simple Report

Tools

DATA _NULL_

FILE and PUT statements

Data

SAS data set CLINICAL

Directions

Using the SAS data set CLINICAL, create a simple report like the one that follows. Use a TITLE statement to create the title and write the report to the OUTPUT window or output device. The three columns of numbers represent ID, systolic blood pressure (SBP), and diastolic blood pressure (DBP).

```
Simple "No Frills" Report
123 136 76
278 104 64
444 128 62
756 150 96
811 166 74
193 112 68
    98 54      Note: There is a missing ID for this observation
978 98 62
586 162 96
919 58 50
  more observations.
```

PROBLEM 2
Adding Header Information and Spacing the Data Values

Tools
DATA _NULL_

FILE PRINT statement

   HEADER= option

PUT statement

Data
SAS data set CLINICAL

Directions
Improve the report in Problem 1 by adding a header which includes the title line and column headings, and space out the data values so that they line up under the headings. The report should look approximately like the one that follows. Do not use a TITLE statement to write the header information. Don't worry about getting the spacing exactly the same as shown here.

```
Listing of Systolic and Diastolic Blood Pressure
   ID          Systolic           Diastolic
            Blood Pressure      Blood Pressure
------------------------------------------------
   123          136                 76
   278          104                 64
   444          128                 62
   756          150                 96
   811          166                 74
   193          112                 68
                 98                 54
   978           98                 62
   586          162                 96
             more observations
```

PROBLEM 3
Customizing a Report

Tools

DATA _NULL_

FILE PRINT statement

    HEADER= option

PUT statement

Either a trailing at sign (@) or SUBSTR pseudo function

Data

SAS data set CLINICAL

Directions

Create a report similar to the one in Problem 2 except place an asterisk (*) after any systolic blood pressure greater than 160 and after any diastolic blood pressure greater than 90. A sample report follows.

Two solutions to this problem are presented in *The SAS Workbook Solutions*. One uses a trailing at sign (@) in the PUT statement along with logical statements to print an asterisk (*) where needed. The other solution creates character variables from SBP and DBP and uses the SUBSTR pseudo function to place an asterisk (*) at the end of the string, if needed. Try to solve this problem both ways.

```
Listing of Systolic and Diastolic Blood Pressure
(Pressures marked with an asterisk (*) are hypertensive)
    ID          Systolic            Diastolic
             Blood Pressure      Blood Pressure
------------------------------------------------
   123           136                  76
   278           104                  64
   444           128                  62
   756           150                  96*
   811           166*                 74
   193           112                  68
                  98                  54
   978            98                  62
   586           162*                 96*
                 etc.
```

Hint

To use the SUBSTR pseudo function you place the function on the left side of the equal sign (=). For example, SUBSTR(STRING,4,1) = '*'.

PROBLEM 4

Creating a Multi-column (Phone Book Style) Report

Tools

    DATA _NULL_

    FILE PRINT statement

        HEADER= and N=PAGESIZE options

    PUT statement

Data

SAS data set CLINICAL

Directions

Again, using the information from the CLINICAL data set, create a report like the one that follows. To help you with alignment, column rulers are placed above the report.

```
         1         2         3         4         5         6         7
1234567890123456789012345678901234567890123456789012345678901234567890
----------------------------------------------------------------------
        Listing of Systolic and Diastolic Blood Pressure

   ID      Systolic  Diastolic     ID      Systolic  Diastolic
              BP        BP                     BP        BP
----------------------------------------------------------------------
  123        136        76        919         58        50
  278        104        64        529        114        76
  444        128        62        324        200       100
  756        150        96        012        184        98
  811        166        74        812        134        82
  193        112        68        338        106        70
              98        54        959        176        98
  978         98        62        007        106        64
  586        162        96        291        132        86
                        more observations
```

SECTION 2

Procedures
(Non-statistical Problems)

CHAPTERS

CHAPTER 12	**The FORMAT Procedure**

PROBLEMS

INTRODUCTION

This chapter covers simple numeric and character formats and informats as well as more complicated problems with control data sets. One of the problems requires you to create a permanent format library and to use the FMTSEARCH= system option indicate where to look for these formats. Other problems use formats as an alternative to writing statements in a DATA step to recode values when you create class variables.

PROBLEM 1
Creating Simple Numeric and Character Formats

Tools
PROC FORMAT

    VALUE statement (discrete ranges)

Data
Raw data described as follows

```
                        Starting
Variable    Description Column    Length   Type
------------------------------------------------------
ID          Subject ID      1        3     Char
GENDER      Gender          4        1     Char
AGEGROUP    Age Group       5        1     Numeric
QUES1       Question 1      6        1     Char
QUES2       Question 2      7        1     Char
QUES3       Question 3      8        1     Char


Sample Data
-----------
001M1123
002F3452
003M2421
004F4531
```

Directions

Given the file description in the Data section, create a SAS data set called SURVEY. Supply formats for GENDER, AGEGROUP, QUES1, QUES2, and QUES3.

```
Format Information for Variables
GENDER          M = Male
                F = Female


AGEGROUP        1 = 0 to 20
                2 = 21 to 40
                3 = 41 to 60
                4 = Greater than 60


QUES1-QUES3     1 = Strongly Disagree
                2 = Disagree
                3 = No Opinion
                4 = Agree
                5 = Strongly Agree
```

PROBLEM 2
Creating Character and Numeric Formats Using Several Methods to Specify Ranges

Tools
PROC FORMAT
  VALUE statement
    LOW and HIGH range keywords

Data
Raw data described as follows

```
                              Starting
     Variable   Description   Column   Length   Type
     ------------------------------------------------
     ID         Subject ID       1        3     Char
     AGE        Age              5        5     Numeric
     CODE       Insurance Code  10        1     Numeric
     PAY        Payment Code    12        1     Char


     Sample Data
     -----------
     001 23.0 1 1
     002 55.9 2 3
     003 60.1 3 2
     004 12.5 1 5
     005 19.1 5 X
```

Directions
Again, you want to supply formats for some variables and create a SAS data set called SURVEY_2. The format information is described next.

```
AGE     Low to <20   = Less than 20
        20 to <40    = 20 to less than 40
        40 to <60    = 40 to less than 60
        60 to high   = 60 and above
Note: Age is expressed to the nearest tenth of a year.
```

```
CODE          1 = Not Insured
              2 = Gold Star Insurance
              3 = Blue Star Insurance
              4 = State Insurance
              5 = Medicare
PAY           1,3,5 = Bill Paid
              2 = 30 Days Overdue
              X,Y = Error in Billing
              4 = Collection Agency
```

PROBLEM 3
Creating Permanent Formats

Tools

PROC FORMAT

   LIBRARY= option

   FMTSEARCH= system option

Data

Same as Problem 1

Directions

Rewrite Problem 1 so that the format you create is made permanent and stored in a subdirectory called C:\WORKBOOK (or another subdirectory of your choice). Run a separate SAS session and submit the appropriate LIBNAME statement so that you can use your permanent formats. When you want to use your permanent formats, either use the libref LIBRARY (in which case the system will find the formats automatically), or use a libref of your choice and tell the system where to find the formats. Use the FMTSEARCH= system option to indicate where to find your formats. Use these permanent formats in a separate SAS session with the data set SURVEY created in Problem 1.

Hint

The two SAS statements that follow create a libref called WORKBOOK and tell the SAS System to search for user-defined formats in this library

```
LIBNAME WORKBOOK 'C:\WORKBOOK';
OPTIONS FMTSEARCH=(WORKBOOK);
```

PROBLEM 4

Using an Existing SAS Data Set to Create a Control Data Set and a User-defined Format (Character Format)

Tools

PROC FORMAT

CNTLIN= and FMTLIB options

Data

SAS data set CODES created by running the following program

```
DATA CODES;
    INPUT @1  DX_CODE $2.
          @4  DESCRIP $16.;
DATALINES;
01 Cold
02 Flu
03 Break or Fracture
04 Routine Physical
05 Heart Problem
06 Lung Disorder
07 Abdominal Pain
08 Laceration
09 Immunization
10 Lyme Disease
11 Ear Ache
;
```

Directions

You have a SAS data set called CODES with variables DX_CODE and DESCRIP. DX_CODE is a 2-byte diagnosis code and DESCRIP is a 16-byte description. Use this data set to create a control data set which can then be used to create a format called $DXFMT. The format associates the DX codes with the descriptions. Run PROC FORMAT to create the format. Use the FMTLIB option to check your format.

PROBLEM 5

Using an Existing SAS Data Set to Create a Control Data Set and a User-defined Format (Numeric Format)

Tools

PROC FORMAT

CNTLIN= option

Data

SAS data set ZIP created by running the following program

```
DATA ZIP;
    INPUT ZIP_CODE LOCATION & $20.;
DATALINES;
08822 Flemington, NJ
11518 East Rockaway, NY
08903 New Brunswick, NJ
;
```

Directions

You have a data set called ZIP with the variables ZIP_CODE (numeric) and LOCATION (character). Use this data set to create a user-defined format (ZIPFMT) by first creating a control data set. Use the FMTLIB option to check your format.

PROBLEM 6

Using an Enhanced Numeric Informat to Read a Combination of Character and Numeric Data

Tools

PROC FORMAT

INVALUE statement (character and numeric ranges)

Data

Blood lead levels as follows

```
5.6 A 2.0 2.1 C 9 B 3.7 X 10
```

Directions

You want to read some blood lead levels from several laboratories. Each laboratory has a detection limit below which they declare the value as a "non-detect." The data are entered with the letters A, B, and C representing the non-detect level for three laboratories. You want to read the blood lead levels and substitute the non-detect level if an A, B, or C is read. The levels corresponding to the letters A through C are

```
Letter Code         Blood Lead Level
------------------------------------
      A                   .1
      B                   .05
      C                   .5
```

Use an "enhanced numeric informat" to read the combination of numbers and letters in the sample line of data and substitute the non-detect levels for the letters A through C. Convert any letters other than A through C to a numeric missing value.

Note

See SAS Technical Report P-222, *Changes and Enhancements to Base SAS Software, Release 6.07,* pp 215-216 for details on the use of the enhanced numeric informat.

PROBLEM 7
Using a Format to Count the Number of Missing Values

Tools

PROC FORMAT

PROC FREQ

   TABLES statement

      MISSING option

NUMERIC, _CHARACTER_, and _ALL_ special SAS variables

Data

SAS data set MISSING created by running the following program

```
DATA MISSING;
    INFILE DATALINES PAD;
    INPUT @1 GROUP $1.
          @3 GENDER $1.
          @5 (X Y Z)(1.+1);
DATALINES;
A M 1 2 3

B F 1   6
A     9 3
M   5 6 7
a f 5 6 7
* $ 9 9 9
;
```

Directions

You have a data set called MISSING. Create two formats, one for the numeric variables and another for the character variables, that you can use with PROC FREQ to count the number of missing and non-missing observations for each of the numeric and character variables.

Note:

1. All upper- and lowercase letters plus the asterisk (*) and the dollar sign ($) are to be considered as valid non-missing character values.

2. Line 2 is blank.

| CHAPTER 13 | The PRINT Procedure |

PROBLEMS

INTRODUCTION

You might think that PROC PRINT is too simple to merit a chapter of its own. However, there are some interesting options and statements that give you quite a bit of control over the appearance of the output. Here are some problems that give you some practice using PROC PRINT.

PROBLEM 1

Preparing a Simple "No-frills" Report

Tools

PROC PRINT

OBS= data set option

VAR and ID statements

Data

SAS data set CLINICAL

Directions

Using the SAS data set CLINICAL, produce a listing of the variables ID, DOB, VISIT, and PRIM_DX for the first ten observations in the data set. Use the variable ID as the leftmost column instead of the default OBS column.

PROBLEM 2

Using Variable Labels as Column Headings

Tools

PROC PRINT

    LABEL= and NOOBS options

    OBS= data set option

    VAR, LABEL, and FORMAT statements

Data

SAS data set CLINICAL

Directions

Repeat Problem 1 but substitute the following labels for the column headings.

```
ID       = 'Patient ID'
DOB      = 'Date of Birth'
VISIT    = 'Date of Visit'
PRIM_DX  = 'Primary DX'
```

Print out both DOB and VISIT using the DATE7. format. Use the NOOBS option, instead of the ID statement, to remove the OBS column from the listing.

Note

Data set CLINICAL already has labels associated with most of the variables, but go ahead and write your own LABEL statement for this problem.

PROBLEM 3

Adding Titles and Footnotes to a Report

Tools

PROC PRINT

    OBS= data set option

    VAR statement

    TITLE and FOOTNOTE statements

Data

SAS data set CLINICAL

Directions

Repeat Problem 1 with the addition of this three-line title

```
Sample Report from the Indian Point Clinic
   (Sample listing of the first ten cases)
   ------------------------------------------
```

and this single-line footnote

```
*** Prepared by Data Systems of Greater Flemington ***
```

PROBLEM 4

Producing a Report Using a BY Variable

Tools

> PROC PRINT
>> BY statement

Data

Raw data file BASKET.DTA

Directions

Create a SAS data set from the raw data file BASKET.DTA. Produce a report separately for males and females, listing all the variables except GENDER (obviously not needed since this is the BY variable). Supply a one-line title of your choosing. Omit the OBS column in the listing.

PROBLEM 5

Using the Value of a BY Variable in a Title

Tools

> PROC PRINT
>> BY and FORMAT statements
>> TITLE statement using #BYVAL (varname)
> NOBYLINE system option

Data

Raw data file BASKET.DTA

Directions

Produce the same report as requested in Problem 4, except add the value of the BY variable (GENDER) to the title and remove the BY line from the report using the NOBYLINE system option. Supply a format for GENDER so that your title reads either

```
Report on the Female Basketball Players
            or
Report on the Male Basketball Players
```

PROBLEM 6

Adding Sums and Counts to a Report

Tools

> PROC PRINT
>> N and LABEL options
>> TITLE statement using #BYVAL (varname)
>> VAR, BY, ID, SUM, LABEL, and FORMAT statements
>> NOBYLINE, NODATE, and NONUMBER system options

Data

Raw data file BASKET.DTA

Directions

Again, using the data from BASKET.DTA, produce a report as follows

- Include the variables GENDER, ID, DATE, and POINTS in the report.

- Print a count of the number of observations for each gender and overall.

- Print the sum of points for males, females, and overall.

- Include the gender information in the title line (and omit the BY line).

- Omit the page number and date from the report using system options.

- Use the WORDDATE. format for the variable DATE.

- Within GENDER, list the IDs in ascending order.

- Use variable labels as column headings as shown in the following report.

```
          The ABC Company Basketball Team Roster
                Data for the Female Players
          ----------------------------------------


   Employee                              Points
   Number              Date              per Game


   002           October 21, 1995           14
   005           December 12, 1995          10
   005           December 15, 1995          18
                                         --------

   GENDER                                    42


                   N = 3

          The ABC Company Basketball Team Roster
                 Data for the Male Players
          ----------------------------------------


   Employee                              Points
   Number              Date              per Game


   001           December 1, 1995           10
   001           December 3, 1995           12
   001           December 10, 1995           8
   003           December 12, 1995          20
   003           December 16, 1995          22
   004           November 12, 1995           6
   004           November 15, 1995           8
   006           October 30, 1995            2
   006           November 4, 1995            6
   006           November 6, 1995            8
   007           November 11, 1995           9
   007           November 16, 1995           7
                                         --------

   GENDER                                   118
                                         ========
                                           160


                   N = 12
             Total N = 15
```

CHAPTER 14 — The SORT Procedure

PROBLEMS

INTRODUCTION

PROC SORT is one of the most frequently used SAS procedures. Like PROC PRINT, it is relatively simple. Since it is used so often and since sorting can take up so much of your system's resources, a brief look at some of its features is very worthwhile. Efficiency matters concerning PROC SORT are discussed in Chapter 20.

PROBLEM I

Sorting in Increasing or Decreasing Order of a Variable

Tools

PROC SORT
  BY statement
    DESCENDING option

Data

Raw data file CARS.DTA

Directions

Using the raw data file CARS.DTA, create a SAS data set called CARS which contains all the variables described in the file but arranged in three different sort orders, as follows.

A. in order of increasing reliability (RELIABLE)

B. in order of decreasing reliability

C. by manufacturer and decreasing size.

For part C, the observations should be ordered by manufacturer (alphabetically). For each manufacturer, the observations should be in decreasing size order. For each of the three sort orders, list the contents of the data set.

PROBLEM 2
Using PROC SORT to Create a New Sorted Data Set

Tools

> PROC SORT
> > OUT= option
> > KEEP= , WHERE=, and LABEL= data set options

Data

SAS data set CLINICAL

Directions

For all the parts below, use only PROC SORT (plus PROC PRINT to list the newly created data set) in your solution. Do not write any DATA steps. As an optional task, use the LABEL data set option to label the newly created data sets.

A. Use PROC SORT to create a new data set called SORTED which contains all the observations and variables in the data set CLINICAL in ascending ID order.

B. Create a new SAS data set called SUBSET1 which contains all the variables in the data set CLINICAL in ascending ID order, but only those patients with SBP above 160.

C. Create a new SAS data set called SUBSET2 which contains all the observations in the data set CLINICAL in ascending ID order, but only the variables ID, SBP, and DBP.

D. Create a new SAS data set called SUBSET3 which contains only patients with SBP above 160. The only variables in SUBSET3 should be ID, SBP, and DBP. This data set should be sorted in increasing order of ID. Provide the label `Clinical data: SBP> 160, ID, and DBP` for the data set SUBSET3.

PROBLEM 3
Removing Records with Duplicate Keys or Duplicate Records

Tools

> PROC SORT
> > NODUP and NODUPKEY options

Data

SAS data set DUP1 and DUP2 created by running the following program

```
DATA DUP1;
   INPUT NAME $ X Y;
DATALINES;
ADAM     2 3
ADAM     2 3
CHARLES  4 7
ADAM     4 5
DAVID    8 9
CHARLES  9 9
;
DATA DUP2;
   INPUT NAME $ X Y;
DATALINES;
ADAM     2 3
CHARLES  4 7
ADAM     4 5
ADAM     2 3
DAVID    8 9
CHARLES  9 9
;
```

Notice that data sets DUP1 and DUP2 contain the same records but in different order.

Directions

Data sets DUP1 and DUP2 contain several observations with the same name and two observations that are identical (that is, they contain the same value for all the variables). Using only PROC SORT (plus PROC PRINT to obtain a listing), accomplish the following tasks.

A. You want only one observation for each name in data set DUP1 (the first observation with that name). Do this using PROC SORT with the appropriate option.

B. This time, you want to remove identical adjacent observations in data set DUP1. That is, one of the two identical observations with NAME=ADAM, X=2, and Y=3 should be removed. Use PROC SORT with the appropriate option to accomplish this.

C. Run the same program as in part B using data set DUP2 instead of DUP1. Notice that after sorting by NAME, the two observations that are identical are not adjacent. Notice which observations (if any) are removed.

D. Figure out a way to remove the non-adjacent identical observations in data set DUP2.

PROBLEM 4
Demonstrating the NOEQUALS Option

Tools

> PROC SORT
>> NOEQUALS option

Data

SAS data set TEST_EQ created by running the following program

```
DATA TEST_EQ;
   INPUT A B @@;
DATALINES;
1 8 1 5 2 5 1 7
;
```

Directions

Sort the data set TEST_EQ by the variable A, creating a new data set called TMP. List the observations in TMP. Sort data set TEST_EQ again using the NOEQUALS option. Again, create an output data set TMP and list the observations. How do the two output data sets compare?

CHAPTER 15

The FREQ Procedure

PROBLEMS

INTRODUCTION

The problems in this chapter include some simple one way frequency tables, two- and *n*-way tables, and problems requiring an output data set from PROC FREQ. For more statistically oriented problems involving PROC FREQ, see Chapter 23 ("Tests of Proportions") in the statistics section of the book.

PROBLEM 1

Producing Simple One-way Frequencies

Tools

PROC FREQ

TABLES statement

Data

Raw data file CARS.DTA

Directions

Using the raw data file CARS.DTA, create a SAS data set and use PROC FREQ to count the number of small, medium and large cars (SIZE) and the frequencies of different manufacturers (MANUFACT).

PROBLEM 2
Producing Simple One-way Frequencies Omitting Percentages and Cumulative Values

---

Tools
PROC FREQ
>TABLES statement
>>NOPERCENT and NOCUM options

Data
Raw data file CARS.DTA

Directions
Repeat Problem 1 except include the options to omit percentages and cumulative values.

PROBLEM 3
Demonstrating how Missing Values Are Handled

Tools
PROC FREQ
>TABLES statement
>>MISSING option

Data
SAS data set CLINICAL

Directions
Using the SAS data set CLINICAL, compute one-way frequencies for the variable SEC_DX. Do this first without the option MISSING on the TABLES statement and then with this option. Compare the two results.

PROBLEM 4
Demonstrating the Effects of the ORDER= Option

Tools
PROC FREQ
>ORDER= option
>>TABLES statement

Data

SAS data set CLINICAL

Directions

Again, using the SAS data set CLINICAL, compute one-way frequencies for the variable PRIM_DX using the ORDER= option with four different values (DATA, FORMATTED, FREQ, and INTERNAL). Compare the results.

PROBLEM 5
Producing Two-way Frequency Tables

Tools

    PROC FREQ

        TABLES statement

            LIST option

Data

Raw data file DEMOG1.DTA

Directions

Using the data from the file DEMOG1.DTA, count the number of males and females (GENDER) that are employed and unemployed (EMPLOYED). Run this with and without the LIST option on the TABLES statement and compare the results.

PROBLEM 6
Requesting Multiple Two-way Tables

Tools

    PROC FREQ

        TABLES statement

Data

Raw data file CPR.DTA

Directions

Using the data from the file CPR.DTA, create three 2 X 2 tables as follows: V_FIB by SURVIVE, RESP by SURVIVE, and AGEGROUP by SURVIVE. Do this with one TABLES statement, making the statement as compact as possible.

PROBLEM 7
Creating an Output Data Set Using PROC FREQ

Tools

PROC FREQ

TABLES statement

OUT= and NOPRINT options

Data

SAS data set CLINICAL

Directions

Use PROC FREQ to create a new data set called COUNTS containing the frequencies of PRIM_DX and SEC_DX from the data set CLINICAL. Provide a listing of this data set.

PROBLEM 8
Producing a Three-way Table

Tools

PROC FREQ

TABLES statement

Data

SAS data set DEMOG1 created in Problem 5

Directions

Using the SAS data set DEMOG1 created in Problem 5, generate a three-way table showing the number of employed (EMPLOYED) males and females (GENDER) for each state (STATE).

PROBLEM 9
Using Formats to Group Variables

Tools

PROC FREQ

PROC FORMAT

Data

SAS data set CARS created in Problem 1

Directions

Using the SAS data set CARS created in Problem 1, produce a table showing the car size (SIZE) by mileage range defined as 0 to 9, 10 to 19, 20 to 29, 30 and above. Create a format for these ranges and add a format statement to PROC FREQ. Do not use a separate data set to create a variable for mileage range.

PROBLEM 10
Using a SAS Format to Group Variables

Tools

PROC FREQ

MONTH. MONNAME3. (WEEKDATE3. or DOWNAME3.) Formats

Data

SAS data set CLINICAL

Directions

Using the SAS data set CLINICAL, compute frequencies for the number of visits per month (try listing the month as a number from 1 to 12 or as a three-letter abbreviation) and the number of visits for each of the days of the week, displayed as a three-letter abbreviation. Do this without using any new DATA steps!

Hint

You will have to run PROC FREQ each time with a different FORMAT statement.

As a special challenge, see if you can list the days of the week (displayed as three-letter abbreviations) in order from Sunday to Saturday. You may need a DATA step to meet this challenge.

CHAPTER 16	The MEANS Procedure

PROBLEMS

INTRODUCTION

This chapter contains non-statistical applications of PROC MEANS. This procedure is useful for counting the number of missing and non-missing observations as well as the more usual computing of means and sums. The problems presented here involve some simple uses of PROC MEANS to produce output listings as well as the slightly more complicated use of PROC MEANS to produce summary output data sets. Now, for the problems.

PROBLEM I

Producing Simple Summary Statistics

Tools

PROC MEANS

MAXDEC= option

N, MEAN, and NMISS statistics keywords

VAR statement

Data

Raw data file CARS.DTA

Directions

Using the raw data file CARS.DTA, create a SAS data set called CARS and compute the number of non-missing observations, the number of missing observations, and the mean for the variables RELIABLE and MILEAGE. Have PROC MEANS print the means to one decimal place.

Note

You may want to include all the variables in the CARS.DTA file when you create your data set since they are needed for other problems in this chapter.

PROBLEM 2
Producing Summary Statistics Broken Down by a Single Variable

Tools

PROC MEANS

MAXDEC= option

N, MEAN, and NMISS statistics keywords

VAR and CLASS statements

Data

SAS data set CARS created in Problem 1

Directions

Rerun Problem 1, except compute the requested statistics for each car SIZE. Use a CLASS statement instead of first sorting the data and using a BY statement.

PROBLEM 3
Creating a Summary Output Data Set with PROC MEANS: One Class Variable

Tools

PROC MEANS

NWAY and NOPRINT options

OUTPUT statement

OUT=, MEAN=, and N= options

DROP= data set option

Data

SAS data set CARS created in Problem 1

Directions

Use PROC MEANS to produce an output data set called CAR_AVE, containing the mean and number of non-missing observations for the variables reliability (RELIABLE) and MILEAGE for each SIZE of car. You only want the _TYPE_ = 1 observations in this data set (i.e., not the mean for all sizes of cars). A PROC MEANS option accomplishes this. Also, use the DROP= data set option to drop the variables _TYPE_ and _FREQ_ from the output data set. Use the variable names M_RELIAB and M_MILE for the means of reliability and mileage. Use the variable names N_RELIAB and N_MILE for the number of non-missing values. Display the contents of this output data set.

PROBLEM 4

Creating a Summary Output Data Set with PROC MEANS: Two Class Variables

---

Tools

    PROC MEANS

        NWAY and NOPRINT options

        OUTPUT statement

        OUT=, MEAN=, and N= options

Data

SAS data set CARS created in Problem 1

Directions

Repeat Problem 3, except create a SAS data set called CAR_MEAN which contains the means and N for every combination of manufacturer (MANUFACT) and SIZE. Use the same variable names for the means and counts as in Problem 3. The output data set should contain only the _TYPE_ = 3 observations. Use a data set option to drop the variables _TYPE_ and _FREQ_ from the output data set. Display the contents of this output data set.

PROBLEM 5
Counting the Number of Missing and Non-missing Values

Tools

> PROC MEANS
> > NOPRINT option
> > OUTPUT statement
> > OUT=, N, and NMISS options
> > DROP= and RENAME= data set options
> PROC PRINT
> > LABEL and NOOBS options

Data

SAS data set MISSING created in Chapter 12, Problem 7

Directions

Repeat Problem 7 in Chapter 12, counting the number of missing and non-missing values for the numeric variables only. Use PROC MEANS, instead of PROC FORMAT, and PROC FREQ to do this. First create an output data set and then use PROC PRINT to print out the results in a listing similar to the following one.

```
          Number of Missing and Non-missing Values

            X        X        Y        Y        Z        Z
Total  Non-missing  Missing  Non-missing  Missing  Non-missing  Missing

  7        5        2        5        2        6        1
```

Note

The variable _FREQ_ has been renamed to TOTAL (and labeled `Total`). The number of non-missing and missing values for the variables X, Y, and Z have been labeled as shown in the listing in the Directions section.

CHAPTER 17 — The TABULATE Procedure

INTRODUCTION

The powerful TABULATE procedure can be used to create multi-way tables of counts, percentages, means, and other statistics. This procedure is thought by some to be difficult to learn. One useful approach is to draw the outlines of the table you want and work backwards to the code. By working your way through the problems that follow, you will gain some proficiency with this extremely useful and not-so-frightening procedure.

All of the problems in this chapter use data from the SAS data set CLINICAL that can be generated by running the program CLINICAL.SAS in the Appendix. Remember that this data set has user-defined formats and labels for many of the variables. For some of the problems, you need to create a new data set which adds the variables MONTH and DAY (of the week), corresponding to the visit date, to the original CLINICAL data set. Finally, the tables shown here are centered on the page with the page numbers and dates omitted from the title line. You may choose to use SAS system options to accomplish this in your output or to use other system options that you prefer.

PROBLEM 1
Creating a Simple One-way Table

Tools

PROC TABULATE

CLASS and TABLE statements

Data

SAS data set CLINICAL

Directions

Using the SAS data set CLINICAL, generate this table.

```
      Simple One-way Table
---------------------------
|         Gender          |
|-------------------------|
|  Female   |    Male     |
|-----------+-------------|
|     N     |     N       |
|-----------+-------------|
|      15.00|       16.00 |
---------------------------
```

PROBLEM 2
Creating a Simple Two-way Table

Tools

PROC TABULATE

CLASS and TABLE statements

ALL class variable

Data

SAS data set CLINICAL

Directions

Using the SAS data set CLINICAL, generate this table.

```
                        Two-way Table
-----------------------------------------------------------------
|                 |  | Pt. Taking Vitamins? |            |
|                 |  |----------------------|            |
|                 |  |   No    |    Yes     |    ALL     |
|                 |  |---------+------------+------------|
|                 |  |    N    |     N      |     N      |
|-----------------+--+---------+------------+------------|
|Gender           |  |         |            |            |
|-----------------|  |         |            |            |
|Female           |  |    6.00 |       9.00 |      15.00 |
|-----------------+--+---------+------------+------------|
|Male             |  |   10.00 |       6.00 |      16.00 |
|-----------------+--+---------+------------+------------|
|ALL              |  |   16.00 |      15.00 |      31.00 |
-----------------------------------------------------------------
```

Note

The column variable is VITAMINS which was given the label `Pt. Taking Vitamins` in the DATA step that created CLINICAL.

PROBLEM 3

Computing Counts and Percentages in a Two-way Table

Tools

> PROC TABULATE
>
> FORMAT= option
>
> CLASS, KEYLABEL, and LABEL statements
>
> TABLE statement
>
> > RTSPACE= option
> >
> > N and PCTN keywords
> >
> > ALL CLASS variable

Data

SAS data set CLINICAL

Directions

Using the SAS data set CLINICAL, generate the table below. Note that the column variable is VITAMINS, and it has been assigned a label. The default table format is 7.0, and the RTSPACE= is set to 25. The KEYLABEL statement assigned the labels All, Number, and Percent to the terms ALL, N, and PCTN, respectively. Notice also that although the variables GENDER and VITAMINS had labels assigned to them in the CLINICAL data set, the table shown here has substituted other labels for these two variables (just to give you practice using a LABEL statement within a procedure).

```
               Counts and Percentages in a Two-way Table
----------------------------------------------------------------------
|                      |           Taking Vitamins?       |          |
|                      |----------------------------------|          |
|                      |     No     |     Yes    |   All  |          |
|                      |-----------------+---------------|          |
|                      |Number |Percent|Number |Percent|Number |Percent|
|----------------------+-------+-------+-------+-------+-------+-------|
|Patient Gender        |       |       |       |       |       |       |
|----------------------|       |       |       |       |       |       |
|Female                |     6 |    19 |     9 |    29 |    15 |    48 |
|----------------------+-------+-------+-------+-------+-------+-------|
|Male                  |    10 |    32 |     6 |    19 |    16 |    52 |
|----------------------+-------+-------+-------+-------+-------+-------|
|All                   |    16 |    52 |    15 |    48 |    31 |   100 |
----------------------------------------------------------------------
```

PROBLEM 4
Selecting a Denominator for a Percentage Calculation

Tools

PROC TABULATE

    FORMAT= option

    CLASS, KEYLABEL, and LABEL statements

    TABLE statement

      RTSPACE= option

      N and PCTN keywords

      ALL class variable

      Brackets (< >) operator (specifies denominator definition)

Data

SAS data set CLINICAL

Directions

Using the SAS data set CLINICAL, create the following table. The default table format is 7.0, and the RTSPACE= option is set to 20. The percentages add up to 100 for the people taking vitamins and the people not taking vitamins. The KEYLABEL statement assigned the labels `All`, `Number`, and `Percent` to the keywords ALL, N, and PCTN, respectively.

```
         Selecting a Denominator for a Percentage
---------------------------------------------------------------
|                 |          Taking Vitamins?     |         |
|                 |-------------------------------|         |
|                 |      No      |     Yes     | All |
|                 |--------------+--------------+-------|
|                 |Number |Percent|Number |Percent|Number |
|-----------------+-------+-------+-------+-------+-------|
|Gender           |       |       |       |       |       |
|-----------------|       |       |       |       |       |
|Female           |      6|     40|      9|     60|     15|
|-----------------+-------+-------+-------+-------+-------|
|Male             |     10|     63|      6|     38|     16|
|-----------------+-------+-------+-------+-------+-------|
|All              |     16|     52|     15|     48|     31|
---------------------------------------------------------------
```

PROBLEM 5

Creating a Three-way Table

Tools

    PROC FORMAT
    PROC TABULATE
        CLASS, LABEL, and KEYLABEL statements
        TABLE statement
            PRINTMISS, BOX=, and MISSTEXT= options
    MONTH and WEEKDAY functions

Data

SAS data set CLINICAL

Directions

Using the SAS data set CLINICAL, create the two following tables. You will need to create a new data set from CLINICAL that contains the month of the year and the day of the week corresponding to the visit date. You will also need to create a format for the month and day abbreviations. The label in the upper left box of each table is the value of the variable GENDER. The keyword N has been labeled `Count`. The labels `Month of Visit` and `Day of Visit` have been assigned to the variables MONTH and DAY, respectively. Missing values are displayed as blanks (not the default period).

```
Three-way Table - Visits by Gender, Month, and Day of Visit
-------------------------------------------------------------
|Gender Female    |             Day of Visit                |
|                 |-----------------------------------------|
|                 | Sun | Mon | Tue | Wed | Thu | Fri | Sat |
|                 |-----+-----+-----+-----+-----+-----+-----|
|                 |Count|Count|Count|Count|Count|Count|Count|
|-----------------+-----+-----+-----+-----+-----+-----+-----|
|Month of Visit   |     |     |     |     |     |     |     |
|-----------------|     |     |     |     |     |     |     |
|Feb              |     |    1|     |     |     |     |     |
|-----------------+-----+-----+-----+-----+-----+-----+-----|
|Mar              |     |     |     |     |     |     |    1|
|-----------------+-----+-----+-----+-----+-----+-----+-----|
|May              |     |    2|    1|     |     |     |     |
|-----------------+-----+-----+-----+-----+-----+-----+-----|
|Jun              |     |     |    1|     |    1|     |     |
|-----------------+-----+-----+-----+-----+-----+-----+-----|
|Jul              |     |     |     |     |     |     |     |
|-----------------+-----+-----+-----+-----+-----+-----+-----|
|Aug              |     |     |    1|    1|     |     |     |
|-----------------+-----+-----+-----+-----+-----+-----+-----|
|Sep              |     |    3|     |     |     |     |     |
|-----------------+-----+-----+-----+-----+-----+-----+-----|
|Oct              |     |     |     |     |     |    1|     |
|-----------------+-----+-----+-----+-----+-----+-----+-----|
|Nov              |     |     |     |     |    1|     |    1|
-------------------------------------------------------------
```

```
Three-way Table - Visits by Gender, Month, and Day of Visit
----------------------------------------------------------------
|Gender Male        |                Day of Visit              |
|                   |------------------------------------------|
|                   | Sun | Mon | Tue | Wed | Thu | Fri | Sat |
|                   |-----+-----+-----+-----+-----+-----+-----|
|                   |Count|Count|Count|Count|Count|Count|Count|
|-------------------+-----+-----+-----+-----+-----+-----+-----|
|Month of Visit     |     |     |     |     |     |     |     |
|-------------------|     |     |     |     |     |     |     |
|Feb                |     |     |     |     |     |     |     |
|-------------------+-----+-----+-----+-----+-----+-----+-----|
|Mar                |     |     |     |     |     |     |     |
|-------------------+-----+-----+-----+-----+-----+-----+-----|
|May                |     |    1|     |     |    2|     |     |
|-------------------+-----+-----+-----+-----+-----+-----+-----|
|Jun                |    1|     |     |     |     |     |    1|
|-------------------+-----+-----+-----+-----+-----+-----+-----|
|Jul                |    2|     |     |    1|     |    1|    1|
|-------------------+-----+-----+-----+-----+-----+-----+-----|
|Aug                |     |     |     |    1|     |     |     |
|-------------------+-----+-----+-----+-----+-----+-----+-----|
|Sep                |     |    1|     |     |     |     |     |
|-------------------+-----+-----+-----+-----+-----+-----+-----|
|Oct                |    1|     |    1|    1|     |     |     |
|-------------------+-----+-----+-----+-----+-----+-----+-----|
|Nov                |     |     |     |     |     |     |    1|
----------------------------------------------------------------
```

PROBLEM 6

Creating a Three-way Table with Percentages

Tools

PROC FORMAT

PROC TABULATE

CLASS, LABEL, and KEYLABEL statements

TABLE statement

PRINTMISS, BOX=, and MISSTEXT= options

N and PCTN keywords

Brackets (< >) operator (specifies denominator definition)

MONTH and WEEKDAY functions

Data

SAS data set CLINICAL

Directions

Using the SAS data set CLINICAL, create the two following tables. They are similar to the tables in Problem 5 with the addition of the percent columns. You will need to create a new data set from CLINICAL (or use the one you created in Problem 5) that contains the month of the year and the day of the week corresponding to the visit date. You will also need to create a format for the month and day abbreviations. The label in the upper left box of each table is the value of the variable GENDER. The keyword N has been labeled N and the keyword PCTN has been labeled %. The labels Month of Visit and Day of Visit have been assigned to the variables MONTH and DAY, respectively. The default table format is 3.0. Missing values are displayed as blanks (not the default period). Note that the percentages add up to 100% for each month.

```
           Three-way Table - Visits by Gender, Month, and Day of Visit
                              Percentages Added
-----------------------------------------------------------------------------
|Gender Female   |                       Day of Visit                       |
|                |----------------------------------------------------------|
|                | Sun  |  Mon  |  Tue  |  Wed  |  Thu  |  Fri  |  Sat  |
|                |------+-------+-------+-------+-------+-------+-------|
|                | N | %| N | %| N | %| N | %| N | %| N | %| N | %|
|----------------+---+--+---+--+---+--+---+--+---+--+---+--+---+--|
|Month of Visit  |   |  |   |  |   |  |   |  |   |  |   |  |   |  |
|----------------|   |  |   |  |   |  |   |  |   |  |   |  |   |  |
|Feb             |   |  | 1|100|   |  |   |  |   |  |   |  |   |  |
|----------------+---+--+---+--+---+--+---+--+---+--+---+--+---+--|
|Mar             |   |  |   |  |   |  |   |  |   |  |   |  | 1|100|
|----------------+---+--+---+--+---+--+---+--+---+--+---+--+---+--|
|May             |   |  | 2| 67| 1| 33|   |  |   |  |   |  |   |  |
|----------------+---+--+---+--+---+--+---+--+---+--+---+--+---+--|
|Jun             |   |  |   |  | 1| 50|   |  | 1| 50|   |  |   |  |
|----------------+---+--+---+--+---+--+---+--+---+--+---+--+---+--|
|Jul             |   |  |   |  |   |  |   |  |   |  |   |  |   |  |
|----------------+---+--+---+--+---+--+---+--+---+--+---+--+---+--|
|Aug             |   |  |   |  | 1| 50| 1| 50|   |  |   |  |   |  |
|----------------+---+--+---+--+---+--+---+--+---+--+---+--+---+--|
|Sep             |   |  | 3|100|   |  |   |  |   |  |   |  |   |  |
|----------------+---+--+---+--+---+--+---+--+---+--+---+--+---+--|
|Oct             |   |  |   |  |   |  |   |  | 1|100|   |  |   |  |
|----------------+---+--+---+--+---+--+---+--+---+--+---+--+---+--|
|Nov             |   |  |   |  |   |  | 1| 50|   |  |   |  | 1| 50|
-----------------------------------------------------------------------------
```

Three-way Table - Visits by Gender, Month, and Day of Visit
Percentages Added

Gender Male		Day of Visit												
		Sun		Mon		Tue		Wed		Thu		Fri		Sat	
		N	%	N	%	N	%	N	%	N	%	N	%	N	%
Month of Visit															
Feb															
Mar															
May				1	33					2	67				
Jun		1	50											1	50
Jul		2	40					1	20			1	20	1	20
Aug								1	100						
Sep				1	100										
Oct		1	33			1	33	1	33						
Nov														1	100

PROBLEM 7
Generating Simple Descriptive Statistics

Tools

PROC TABULATE

VAR, TABLE, KEYLABEL, and LABEL statements

Specifying individual formats for table elements

N, NMISS, MEAN, STD, MIN, and MAX statistics keywords

Data

SAS data set CLINICAL

Directions

Using the SAS data set CLINICAL, create the following table. The row variables are HR, SBP, and DBP. The default table format is 8.0, and formats for N, MEAN, and STD are 7.0, 6.1, and 6.2, respectively. The keywords N, NMISS, MEAN, STD, MIN, and MAX have been labeled `Number`, `Missing`, `Mean`, `S.D.`, `Minimum`, and `Maximum`, respectively. The RTSPACE= option is set to 20.

```
                     Basic Descriptive Statistics

---------------------------------------------------------------------------
|                 |Number |Missing | Mean | S.D. |Minimum |Maximum |
|-----------------+-------+--------+------+------+--------+--------|
|Heart Rate       |    30|      1|  78.5| 10.17|     58|     92|
|-----------------+-------+--------+------+------+--------+--------|
|Systolic BP      |    30|      1| 134.0| 39.91|     54|    220|
|-----------------+-------+--------+------+------+--------+--------|
|Diastolic BP     |    30|      1|  82.9| 27.50|     36|    180|
---------------------------------------------------------------------------
```

PROBLEM 8

Producing Simple Descriptive Statistics Broken Down by a Single Variable (Statistics Nested within the Row Variable)

Tools

PROC TABULATE

VAR, CLASS, TABLE, KEYLABEL, and LABEL statements

Specifying individual formats for table elements

N, MEAN, STD, and STDERR statistics keywords

Data

SAS data set CLINICAL

Directions

Using the SAS data set CLINICAL, create the following table. The row variables are HR, SBP, and DBP. No formats are specified. The keywords N, MEAN, STD, STDERR, and the class variable ALL have been labeled `Number`, `Mean`, `S.D.`, `S.E.`, and `All`, respectively. The RTSPACE= option is set to 30. The labels `Heart Rate`, `Systolic BP`, `Diastolic BP`, and `Gender` have been assigned to the variables HR, SBP, DBP, and GENDER, respectively.

```
Simple Statistics Broken Down by a Single Variable
-----------------------------------------------------------------------
|                        |              Gender            |           |
|                        |--------------------------------|           |
|                        |   Female   |    Male   |    All            |
|------------------------+------------+-----------+-----------|
|Heart Rate  |Number     |      15.00|      15.00|      30.00|
|            |-----------+------------+-----------+-----------|
|            |Mean       |      81.33|      75.67|      78.50|
|            |-----------+------------+-----------+-----------|
|            |S.D.       |       8.44|      11.21|      10.17|
|            |-----------+------------+-----------+-----------|
|            |S.E.       |       2.18|       2.89|       1.86|
|------------+-----------+------------+-----------+-----------|
|Systolic BP |Number     |      15.00|      15.00|      30.00|
|            |-----------+------------+-----------+-----------|
|            |Mean       |     130.53|     137.47|     134.00|
|            |-----------+------------+-----------+-----------|
|            |S.D.       |      46.44|      33.42|      39.91|
|            |-----------+------------+-----------+-----------|
|            |S.E.       |      11.99|       8.63|       7.29|
|------------+-----------+------------+-----------+-----------|
|Diastolic BP|Number     |      15.00|      15.00|      30.00|
|            |-----------+------------+-----------+-----------|
|            |Mean       |      74.13|      91.60|      82.87|
|            |-----------+------------+-----------+-----------|
|            |S.D.       |      21.32|      30.79|      27.50|
|            |-----------+------------+-----------+-----------|
|            |S.E.       |       5.50|       7.95|       5.02|
-----------------------------------------------------------------------
```

PROBLEM 9

Producing Simple Descriptive Statistics Broken Down by a Single Variable (Statistics Nested within the Column Variable)

Tools

PROC TABULATE

VAR, CLASS, TABLE, KEYLABEL, and LABEL statements

Specifying individual formats for table elements

N, MEAN, STD, and STDERR statistics keywords

Data

SAS data set CLINICAL

Directions

Using the SAS data set CLINICAL, create the following table. Notice that the information contained in this table is similar to that in Problem 8, except that the standard error is omitted and the statistics are now displayed within each value of GENDER. Formats for the statistics N, MEAN, and STD are 6.0, 5.1, and 5.2, respectively. The labels for statistics and variables are identical to the labels in Problem 8. The RTSPACE= option is set to 15.

```
         Simple Statistics Broken Down by a Single Variable
-----------------------------------------------------------------------
|              |               Gender                |               |
|              |-------------------------------------|               |
|              |    Female    |     Male     |     ALL                |
|              |-----------------+-----------------+-----------------|
|              |Number|Mean |S.D. |Number|Mean |S.D. |Number|Mean |S.D. |
|-------------+------+-----+-----+------+-----+-----+------+-----+-----|
|Heart Rate   |    15| 81.3| 8.44|    15| 75.7|11.21|    30| 78.5|10.17|
|-------------+------+-----+-----+------+-----+-----+------+-----+-----|
|Systolic BP  |    15|130.5|46.44|    15|137.5|33.42|    30|134.0|39.91|
|-------------+------+-----+-----+------+-----+-----+------+-----+-----|
|Diastolic BP |    15| 74.1|21.32|    15| 91.6|30.79|    30| 82.9|27.50|
-----------------------------------------------------------------------
```

PROBLEM 10

Producing Simple Descriptive Statistics Broken Down by a Single Variable (Breakdown Variable Nested within the Computation Variable)

Tools

    PROC TABULATE
        VAR, CLASS, KEYLABEL, and LABEL statements
        TABLE statement
            RTSPACE=, PRINTMISS, and BOX= options
        Specifying individual formats for table elements
        N, MEAN, NMISS, MEAN, STD, MIN, and MAX statistics keywords

Data

SAS data set CLINICAL

Directions

Using the SAS data set CLINICAL, create the following table. The keywords N, NMISS, MEAN, STD, MIN, and MAX have been assigned labels `Number`, `Missing`, `Mean`, `S.D.`, `Minimum`, and `Maximum`, respectively. The text `Place Your Ad Here` is inserted in the upper left-hand box. The default table format is 8.0, and formats for the statistics N, MEAN, and STD are 7.0, 6.1, and 6.2, respectively. The RTSPACE= option is set to 28.

```
                 Basic Descriptive Statistics
                   Broken Down by Gender
-----------------------------------------------------------------------
|Place Your Ad Here      |Number |Missing | Mean | S.D. |Minimum |Maximum |
|------------------------+-------+--------+------+------+--------+--------|
|Heart Rate  |Gender     |       |        |      |      |        |        |
|            |-----------|       |        |      |      |        |        |
|            |Female     |    15 |     0  | 81.3 | 8.44 |     68 |     92 |
|            |-----------+-------+--------+------+------+--------+--------|
|            |Male       |    15 |     1  | 75.7 |11.21 |     58 |     88 |
|            |-----------+-------+--------+------+------+--------+--------|
|            |Total      |    30 |     1  | 78.5 |10.17 |     58 |     92 |
|------------+-----------+-------+--------+------+------+--------+--------|
|Systolic BP |Gender     |       |        |      |      |        |        |
|            |-----------|       |        |      |      |        |        |
|            |Female     |    15 |     0  |130.5 |46.44 |     54 |    200 |
|            |-----------+-------+--------+------+------+--------+--------|
|            |Male       |    15 |     1  |137.5 |33.42 |     98 |    220 |
|            |-----------+-------+--------+------+------+--------+--------|
|            |Total      |    30 |     1  |134.0 |39.91 |     54 |    220 |
|------------+-----------+-------+--------+------+------+--------+--------|
|Diastolic BP|Gender     |       |        |      |      |        |        |
|            |-----------|       |        |      |      |        |        |
|            |Female     |    15 |     0  | 74.1 |21.32 |     36 |    110 |
|            |-----------+-------+--------+------+------+--------+--------|
|            |Male       |    15 |     1  | 91.6 |30.79 |     62 |    180 |
|            |-----------+-------+--------+------+------+--------+--------|
|            |Total      |    30 |     1  | 82.9 |27.50 |     36 |    180 |
-----------------------------------------------------------------------
```

PROBLEM 11

Statistics Broken Down by Two Variables

Tools

PROC TABULATE

    CLASS, VAR, KEYLABEL, and LABEL statements

    TABLE statement

        RTSPACE= and PRINTMISS options

Data

SAS data set CLINICAL

Directions

Using the SAS data set CLINICAL, create the following table. The labels `Number`, `Mean`, and `Both` have been assigned to statistics N, MEAN, and ALL, respectively. The variables HR, SBP, and DBP are labeled `Heart Rate`, `Systolic BP`, and `Diastolic BP`, respectively. The row variables are VITAMINS and GENDER. The format for N is 6.0, and the format for MEAN is 5.1.

```
            Simple Statistics Broken Down by Two Variables
-----------------------------------------------------------------------------
|                                  | Heart Rate |Systolic BP |Diastolic BP|
|                                  |------------+------------+------------|
|                                  |Number|Mean |Number|Mean |Number|Mean |
|----------------------------------+------+-----+------+-----+------+-----|
|Taking Vitamins? |Gender          |      |     |      |     |      |     |
|-----------------+----------------|      |     |      |     |      |     |
|No               |Female          |    6| 82.0|     6|150.0|    6| 84.0|
|                 |----------------+------+-----+------+-----+------+-----|
|                 |Male            |   10| 75.1|    10|142.6|   10| 98.8|
|                 |----------------+------+-----+------+-----+------+-----|
|                 |Both            |   16| 77.7|    16|145.4|   16| 93.3|
|-----------------+----------------+------+-----+------+-----+------+-----|
|Yes              |Gender          |      |     |      |     |      |     |
|                 |----------------|      |     |      |     |      |     |
|                 |Female          |    9| 80.9|     9|117.6|    9| 67.6|
|                 |----------------+------+-----+------+-----+------+-----|
|                 |Male            |    5| 76.8|     5|127.2|    5| 77.2|
|                 |----------------+------+-----+------+-----+------+-----|
|                 |Both            |   14| 79.4|    14|121.0|   14| 71.0|
|-----------------+----------------+------+-----+------+-----+------+-----|
|Both             |Gender          |      |     |      |     |      |     |
|                 |----------------|      |     |      |     |      |     |
|                 |Female          |   15| 81.3|    15|130.5|   15| 74.1|
|                 |----------------+------+-----+------+-----+------+-----|
|                 |Male            |   15| 75.7|    15|137.5|   15| 91.6|
|                 |----------------+------+-----+------+-----+------+-----|
|                 |Both            |   30| 78.5|    30|134.0|   30| 82.9|
-----------------------------------------------------------------------------
```

CHAPTER 18 — The CHART Procedure

INTRODUCTION

Although you can make fancy, publication-quality charts using SAS/GRAPH software, PROC CHART still serves a useful purpose. It is fast, easy to use, and it produces useful displays of one or more variables.

PROBLEM 1
Creating a Vertical Bar Chart to Display Frequencies (Character Variables)

Tools

PROC CHART
VBAR statement

Data
Raw data file CARS.DTA

Directions
Using the raw data file CARS.DTA (or the SAS data set created in Chapter 2, Problem 1), create two vertical bar charts showing the frequencies for the variables SIZE and MANUFACT.

PROBLEM 2
Creating a Horizontal Bar Chart to Display Frequencies (Character Variables)

Tools

PROC CHART

    HBAR statement

        NOSTAT option

Data

Raw data file CARS.DTA or SAS data set CARS from Problem 1

Directions

Repeat Problem 1, but this time produce horizontal bar charts. Do this first with the default statistics and then with the NOSTAT option to delete the statistics.

PROBLEM 3
Creating a Bar Chart Displaying Percentages

Tools

PROC CHART

    VBAR statement

        TYPE=PERCENT option

Data

Raw data file CARS.DTA or SAS data set CARS from Problem 1

Directions

Using data from the raw data file CARS.DTA or the SAS data set created in Problem 1, create a single vertical bar chart showing the percentages of cars of each SIZE.

PROBLEM 4
Creating a Bar Chart for a Numeric Variable (Discrete Values)

Tools

PROC CHART

    VBAR statement

        DISCRETE option

Data

Raw data file CARS.DTA or SAS data set CARS from Problem 1

Directions

Using data from the raw data file CARS.DTA or the SAS data set created in Problem 1, produce a vertical bar chart showing the frequencies of reliability ratings (RELIABLE). The values for the variable RELIABLE should be the integers 1 to 5.

PROBLEM 5

Creating a Bar Chart for a Numeric Variable Using a Variety of Methods for Choosing Midpoints

---

Tools

> PROC CHART
>> VBAR statement
>>> MIDPOINTS= and LEVELS= options

Data

Raw data file CARS.DTA or SAS data set CARS from Problem 1

Directions

Using data from the raw data file CARS.DTA or the SAS data set created in Problem 1, produce vertical bar charts for the variable MILEAGE that employ

A. system-chosen (default) midpoints

B. the MIDPOINTS= option to select the following midpoints: 15, 20, 25, 30, 35, and 40

C. the LEVELS= option to generate five bars.

PROBLEM 6

Creating a Bar Chart Displaying Sums of One Variable for Different Values of Another Variable

---

Tools

> PROC CHART
>> VBAR statement
>>> SUMVAR= and TYPE= options

Data

Raw data file BASKET.DTA

Directions

Using the BASKET.DTA data file, create a SAS data set and display the total number of POINTS for males and females in a vertical chart.

PROBLEM 7

Representing Two Variables on a Single Chart

Tools

PROC CHART

VBAR statement

GROUP= and DISCRETE options

Data

Raw data file CARS.DTA or SAS data set CARS from Problem 1

Directions

Using data from the CARS.DTA data file or the SAS data set created in Problem 1, create a vertical bar chart showing the distribution of the reliability index (RELIABLE) for each size of car (SIZE). Your chart should look like the following one.

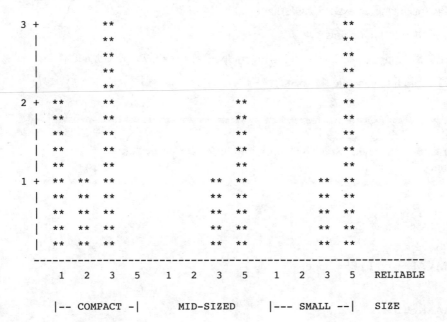

```
Reliability by Car Size


Frequency


3 +           **                          **
  |           **                          **
  |           **                          **
  |           **                          **
  |           **                          **
2 +   **      **                  **       **
  |   **      **                  **       **
  |   **      **                  **       **
  |   **      **                  **       **
  |   **      **                  **       **
1 +   **  **  **          **  **  **  **
  |   **  **  **          **  **  **  **
  |   **  **  **          **  **  **  **
  |   **  **  **          **  **  **  **
  |   **  **  **          **  **  **  **
      ----------------------------------------------------------
       1   2   3   5   1   2   3   5   1   2   3   5   RELIABLE

      |-- COMPACT -|     MID-SIZED    |--- SMALL --|   SIZE
```

Notes

1. There are no cars with a value of 4 for reliability. Treat the values of reliability (RELIABLE) as discrete values in your procedure.

2. System options PS=48 and LS=74 were used to produce this chart and the remaining charts in this chapter.

PROBLEM 8
Using the Value of a Variable as a Charting Symbol

Tools

> PROC CHART
>> VBAR statement
>>> SUBGROUP= option

Data

Raw data file CARS.DTA or SAS data set CARS from Problem 1

Directions

Using data from the CARS.DTA data file or the SAS data set created in Problem 1, display the frequency distribution showing the number of cars for each manufacturer. Use the first character of the variable SIZE to draw the bars. Your chart should look like the following one.

```
Distribution by Manufacturer and Car Size


Frequency

3 +                     SSSS
  |                     SSSS
  |                     SSSS
  |                     SSSS
  |                     SSSS
2 +       SSSS          MMMM  SSSS          SSSS
  |       SSSS          MMMM  SSSS          SSSS
  |       SSSS          MMMM  SSSS          SSSS
  |       SSSS          MMMM  SSSS          SSSS
  |       SSSS          MMMM  SSSS          SSSS
```

```
1 +  CCCC  CCCC  CCCC  SSSS  CCCC  MMMM  CCCC  CCCC  MMMM
  |   CCCC  CCCC  CCCC  SSSS  CCCC  MMMM  CCCC  CCCC  MMMM
  |   CCCC  CCCC  CCCC  SSSS  CCCC  MMMM  CCCC  CCCC  MMMM
  |   CCCC  CCCC  CCCC  SSSS  CCCC  MMMM  CCCC  CCCC  MMMM
  |   CCCC  CCCC  CCCC  SSSS  CCCC  MMMM  CCCC  CCCC  MMMM
      --------------------------------------------------------
          B     C     C     D     F     H     P     P     T
          U     H     H     O     O     O     L     O     O
          I     E     R     D     R     N     Y     N     Y
          C     V     Y     G     D     D     M     T     O
          K     R     S     E           A     O     I     T
                O     L                       U     A     A
                L     E                       T     C
                E     R                       H
                T

                         MANUFACT

Symbol SIZE          Symbol SIZE          Symbol SIZE

   C    COMPACT          M    MID-SIZED        S    SMALL
```

PROBLEM 9

Creating a Three-dimensional Chart

Tools

PROC CHART

BLOCK statement

GROUP=, SUMVAR=, and TYPE= options

Data

Raw data file CARS.DTA or SAS data set CARS from Problem 1

Directions

Using data from the CARS.DTA data file or the SAS data set created in Problem 1, create a three-dimensional chart showing the average (mean) gas mileage (z-axis) for each level of reliability (x-axis) and SIZE (y-axis). The block chart should look like the following one.

Three-Dimensional Block Chart

Mean of MILEAGE by RELIABLE grouped by SIZE

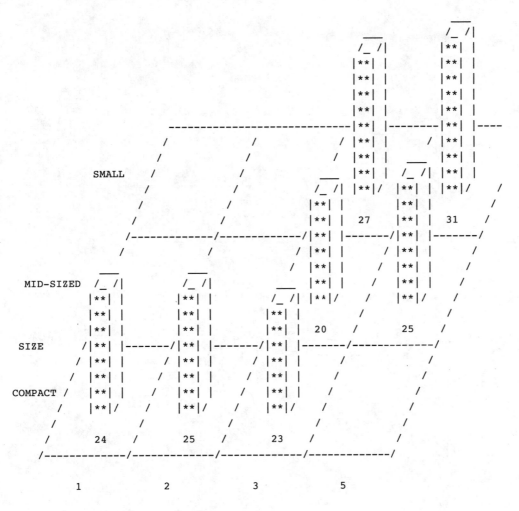

RELIABLE

CHAPTER 19 | The PLOT Procedure

PROBLEMS

INTRODUCTION

If you need high-quality, camera-ready graphs, you should consider using a SAS/GRAPH procedure. However, PROC PLOT is useful and easy to use. It can give you a quick plot showing relationships between variables. With a few simple statements, you can select plotting symbols and label points on the plot.

PROBLEM I

Producing a Simple X-Y Plot: Selecting Plotting Symbols

Tools

> PROC PLOT
>> PLOT statement
>>> Plotting symbol

Data

SAS data set CLINICAL

Directions

Using the SAS data set CLINICAL, do the following

A. Plot SBP (y-axis) by HR (x-axis) using the default plotting symbol.

B. Rerun (A) using a lowercase o as the plotting symbol.

C. Rerun (A) using the value of GENDER as the plotting symbol.

PROBLEM 2
Requesting Multiple Plots

Tools

PROC PLOT
> PLOT statement
>> OVERLAY option

Data

SAS data set CLINICAL

Directions

Using the SAS data set CLINICAL, produce the following plots.

A. Two separate plots: one of SBP (y-axis) by HR (x-axis), the other DBP (y-axis) by HR (x-axis). Use the default plotting symbol.

B. The same two plots as in (A), but plot both graphs on the same set of axes. Use the letter S as the plotting symbol for the SBP by HR plot and the letter D as the plotting symbol for the DBP by HR plot.

PROBLEM 3
Labeling Points on a Scatter Plot

Tools

PROC PLOT
> PLOT statement
>> Label variable

Data

SAS data set CLINICAL

Directions

Using the SAS data set CLINICAL, produce a plot of SBP (y-axis) by HR (x-axis). Label each point with the patient's diagnosis (PRIM_DX), and use a lowercase o as the plotting symbol. Use SAS system options to set the pagesize to 48 and the linesize to 64.

Note

See page 230 in SAS Technical Report P-222, *Changes and Enhancements to Base SAS Software, Release 6.07.*

PROBLEM 4
Labeling Points on a Scatter Plot and Using the Value of a Variable as a Plotting Symbol

Tools

PROC PLOT

PLOT statement

Labeling feature

PAGESIZE= , LINESIZE= , and PAGENO= system options

Data

SAS data set LEAD created by running the following program

```
DATA LEAD;
   INPUT LAB $ SUBJECT $ LEVEL_1 LEVEL_2;
   LABEL LEVEL_1 = 'Lead at Time 1'
         LEVEL_2 = 'Lead at Time 2';
DATALINES;
Carter 1 3 3
Carter 2 6 6.5
Carter 3 9 9.5
H&K 1 3.5 3
H&K 2 7 7
H&K 3 10 10
Boston 1 1 2
Boston 2 5 6
Boston 3 7 6
;
```

Directions

A study was conducted to test the consistency of laboratories in measuring blood lead levels. Each of three subjects had blood drawn. Two samples were sent to each of three different laboratories, one immediately after being drawn and the other one a week later. Using the SAS data set LEAD created in the Data section, produce a scatter plot of LEVEL_2 (y-axis) by LEVEL_1 (x-axis) with the subject number as the plotting symbol. Label the points with the value of the variable LAB. Set the pagesize to 24, the linesize to 64, and the page number to 1.

To help you understand what is required for this problem, see the following plot.

Lead Levels at Time 1 and Time 2 by Lab and Subject

Plot of LEVEL_2*LEVEL_1$LAB. Symbol is value of SUBJECT.

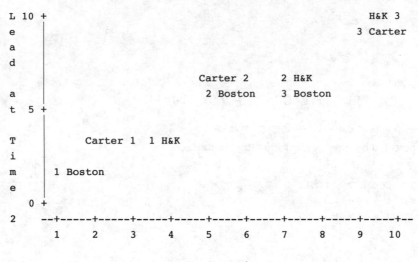

```
L 10 +                                                    H&K 3
e    |                                                    3 Carter
a    |
d    |
a    |                        Carter 2      2 H&K
t  5 +                        2 Boston      3 Boston
     |
T    |
i    |           Carter 1   1 H&K
m    |
e    |  1 Boston
   0 +
2    --+-----+-----+-----+-----+-----+-----+-----+-----+-----+--
       1     2     3     4     5     6     7     8     9     10
```

Lead at Time 1

SECTION 3 | SAS® Programming Techniques

CHAPTER 20 — Efficient Programming

INTRODUCTION

Each of the problems in this chapter can be written more efficiently. There are times when a "quick and dirty" program works fine, but learning and practicing the basic concepts of efficient programming can reduce CPU time, disk access time, or both.

Some of the problems use the SAS data set CLINICAL. However, since it is such a small data set, you may not notice any difference in execution time between the inefficient and efficient versions of the programs. Therefore, I have provided the SAS code to generate two larger data sets, EFF1 (10,000 observations and 5 variables) and EFF2 (1,000 observations and 100 variables). To test programs that read raw data, I have also provided a program to create raw data file RAWDATA with 10,000 observations and 10 variables.

Remember that some of the "rules" for efficient programming change with newer releases of the SAS System and may depend on which computer or operating environment you are using. See the Problem title and the Tools list for hints on how to approach each problem. Finally, if you plan to "benchmark" each of the inefficient programs in this chapter with your more efficient version, you may need to turn off, or take into account, any disk-caching software you may be running (i.e., SMARTDISK with Microsoft Windows).

Here are the programs to create data sets EFF1 and EFF2 and the raw data file RAWDATA.

```
*-----------------------------------------------*
| Program to create SAS data set EFF1           |
*-----------------------------------------------*;
DATA EFF1;
   LENGTH X Y P1 P2 4 GROUP $ 1;
   DO I = 1 TO 10000;
       X  = RANUNI(1357);
       Y  = RANUNI(2468);
       P1 = (X LT .5);
       P2 = (Y LT .001);
       IF X > .8 THEN GROUP = 'A';
       ELSE IF X > .6 THEN GROUP = 'B';
       ELSE IF X > .4 THEN GROUP = 'C';
       ELSE GROUP = 'D';
       OUTPUT;
   END;
   DROP I;
RUN;


*-----------------------------------------------*
| Program to create SAS data set EFF2           |
*-----------------------------------------------*;
DATA EFF2;
   ARRAY X[100] X1-X100;
   DO I = 1 TO 1000;
      DO J = 1 TO 100;
          X[J] = RANUNI(1357);
      END;
      OUTPUT;
   END;
DROP I J;
RUN;


*-----------------------------------------------*
| Program to create data file RAWDATA           |
*-----------------------------------------------*;
DATA _NULL_;
   FILE 'C:\WORKBOOK\RAWDATA';  ***Use a subdirectory of your choice
here;
```

```
    LENGTH GROUP $ 1;
    ARRAY X[10] X1-X10;
    DO I = 1 TO 10000;
        DO J = 1 TO 10;
            X[J] = RANUNI(1357);
        END;
        IF X1 > .99 THEN GROUP = 'A';
        ELSE GROUP = 'B';
        PUT @1 (X1-X10) (5.3 + 1) @65 GROUP $1.;
    END;
RUN;
```

PROBLEM I
Avoiding Unnecessary DATA Steps

Tools

DATA= option

WHERE statement or WHERE= data set option

Data

SAS data set EFF1

Directions

Rewrite the following program to make it more efficient. Do not use a DATA step.

```
DATA NEW;
    SET EFF1; *** or libref.EFF1 if you made it permanent;
    WHERE P2 = 1;
RUN;

PROC MEANS N MEAN MAXDEC=2 DATA=NEW;
    TITLE 'Descriptive Statistics on X and Y';
    VAR X Y;
RUN;
```

PROBLEM 2
Avoiding Unnecessary Sorts

Tools
    PROC MEANS
        CLASS statement

Data
SAS data set EFF1

Directions
Rewrite the following program, eliminating the need to sort the data set.

```
PROC SORT DATA=EFF1 OUT=TMP;
   BY GROUP;
RUN;


PROC MEANS DATA=TMP N MEAN;
   BY GROUP;
RUN;
```

PROBLEM 3
Sorting Only What You Need

Tools
    PROC SORT
        KEEP= and WHERE= data set options

Data
SAS data set EFF2

Directions
Rewrite the following program to make it more efficient.

```
PROC SORT DATA=EFF2 OUT=OUT1;
   BY X1;
RUN;

DATA SUBSET;
   SET OUT1;
   WHERE X1 > .9;
   KEEP X1;
RUN;
```

PROBLEM 4
Using KEEP Statements

Tools
KEEP statement

MEAN function

Data
SAS data set EFF2

Directions
Rewrite the following program to make it more efficient.

```
DATA DESCRIP;
   SET EFF2;
   MEAN = MEAN (OF X1-X100);
RUN;
```

Note
Only the variable MEAN is needed in the new data set.

PROBLEM 5
Using DATA_NULL_ when a Data Set Is Not Needed

Tools
DATA _NULL_

FILE statement

Data
SAS data set CLINICAL

Directions
Rewrite the following program to make it more efficient.

```
LIBNAME WORKBOOK 'C:\WORKBOOK';
OPTIONS FMTSEARCH=(WORKBOOK);
```

```
DATA REPORT;
   SET WORKBOOK.CLINICAL;
   FILE PRINT;
   IF SBP > 160 OR DBP > 90 THEN
      PUT ID= SBP= DBP=;
RUN;
```

Note

You have no plans to use data set REPORT for anything.

PROBLEM 6
Using LENGTH Statements where Possible (Numeric Example)

Tools
   LENGTH statement

Data
SAS data set EFF2

Directions
Rewrite the following program to make it more efficient. For this example, assume that a precision of 4 bytes for the numeric variables is sufficient.

```
DATA SUBSET;
   SET EFF2;
   WHERE X1 > .5;
RUN;
```

Note
Some SAS users recommend never using numeric lengths of fewer than 8 bytes. In the right situation, with proper care, you may be fine using shorter lengths. For more information, see the section on numeric values in Chapter 3, "Components of the SAS Language," in *SAS Language: Reference, Version 6, First Edition.*

PROBLEM 7

Using LENGTH Statements to Control the Length of Character Variables

Tools

LENGTH statement

Data

Located in the inefficient program example in the Directions section

Directions

Rewrite the following program so that the length of character variables are as short as possible. (The length of the variables A, B, C, and LETTER should be one byte and GROUP should be set to seven bytes.) You should run the inefficient program first and then run PROC CONTENTS to see the lengths assigned to these variables.

```
DATA LONGCHAR;
   INPUT A $ B $ C $ GROUP $;
   LETTER = SUBSTR(GROUP,1,1);
DATALINES;
1 0 1 CONTROL
0 0 0 TREAT
1 1 1 CONTROL
1 0 1 TREAT
0 1 1 TREAT
;
```

PROBLEM 8

Using PROC FORMAT to Regroup Variables

Tools

PROC FORMAT
PROC FREQ

Data

SAS data set EFF1

Directions

Rewrite the following program, using PROC FORMAT to regroup the values of X and using a FORMAT statement in PROC FREQ to accomplish your goal. Do not use a DATA step at all. This may not be efficient if you plan to use these groupings more than once and want to store them in a permanent data set. However, for this problem, assume that your disk space is limited and that you do not want to create a new data set.

```
DATA GROUP;
   SET EFF1;
   IF 0 LE X LT .2 THEN RANGE = 1;
   ELSE IF .2 LE X LT .4 THEN RANGE = 2;
   ELSE IF .4 LE X LT .6 THEN RANGE = 3;
   ELSE IF .6 LE X LT .8 THEN RANGE = 4;
   ELSE IF .8 LE X LE 1  THEN RANGE = 5;
RUN;

PROC FREQ DATA=GROUP;
   TABLES RANGE;
RUN;
```

PROBLEM 9
Using a KEEP= Data Set Option instead of a KEEP Statement

Tools

KEEP= data set option

KEEP statement

Data

SAS data set EFF2

Directions

Rewrite the following program to make it more efficient.

```
DATA SUBSET;
   SET EFF2;
   IF 0 LE X1 LE .5 THEN PROP = 0;
      ELSE PROP = 1;
   KEEP PROP;
RUN;
```

Hint

Data set EFF2 contains 100 variables, X1-X100, and you only need to have a single variable, PROP, in the data set SUBSET.

PROBLEM 10
Using an Index to Increase Efficiency

Tools

PROC DATASETS
    INDEX CREATE statement
PROC FREQ
    WHERE statement

Data

SAS data set EFF1

Directions

Make the following program more efficient by using PROC DATASETS to create an index for the variable P2 before running PROC FREQ. When you are finished, use PROC DATASETS to remove the index.

```
PROC FREQ DATA=EFF1;
   TITLE 'Where Processing - No Index Used';
   WHERE P2 = 1;
   TABLES GROUP;
RUN;
```

Note

An index will not always improve the efficiency of your program. You may want to run some tests to see if there is improvement. In preparing this problem, some programs ran slower with an indexed variable than without. You may also want to consider the time it takes to create the index, although the index only needs to be created once.

PROBLEM 11
Reading Only What You Need to from Raw Data

Tools

Trailing at sign (@)

Data

Located in the inefficient example in the Directions section

Directions

The following program reads the data file RAWDATA and creates a subset of the observations. Rewrite this program to make it more efficient.

```
DATA SUBSET;
   INFILE 'C:\WORKBOOK\RAWDATA'; *** The location of RAWDATA;
   INPUT @1  (X1-X10) (5.3 + 1)
         @65 GROUP $1.;
   IF GROUP = 'A';
RUN;
```

PROBLEM 12

Arranging the Order of IF and IF-THEN/ELSE Statements

Tools

   IF-THEN/ELSE statement

Data

SAS data set EFF1

Directions

If you know the relative frequency of values in a data set, you can arrange the IF and IF-THEN/ELSE statements so that the statements more likely to be true appear earlier in the list. In data set EFF1, the value of P2 is 0 for most observations. Rewrite the following program so that it runs more efficiently.

```
DATA NEW;
   SET EFF1;
   IF P2 = 1 THEN NEWVAR = X;
        ELSE NEWVAR = Y;
RUN;
```

CHAPTER 21

PROBLEMS

INTRODUCTION

Problems in this chapter are longer than problems elsewhere in the book and may require quite a few DATA step techniques and SAS procedures. The Tools lists do not include all the things you need to solve the problem; they do list suggestions on some techniques that may be useful.

PROBLEM 1

Working with Longitudinal Data

Tools

FIRST.*variable* and LAST.*variable* temporary variables

PROC MEANS

OUTPUT statement

Data

Raw data file CLIN_X.DTA

Directions

A. Using the raw data file CLIN_X.DTA, create a permanent SAS data set called CLIN_X. Locate the data set in a subdirectory on your hard disk, on a floppy disk, or in another location appropriate to your version of SAS software and operating environment. Provide permanent formats (to be stored in the same library as the permanent data set) and labels.

B. Create a temporary SAS data set (LAST) which contains only the last visit for each patient.

C. For the variables HR, SBP, and DBP in the LAST data set, compute the number of non-missing observations, the mean, and the standard deviation. Compute these statistics to two decimal places.

D. Using the CLIN_X data set, compute the mean HR, SBP, and DBP for each patient and output these values (along with the patient ID) to a SAS data set called MEANS. Use this MEANS data set to compute the mean HR, SBP, and DBP. That is, compute the mean of the patient means.

E. Compute frequencies for diagnosis codes (DX) and treatments (RX_1 and RX_2). Remember that each patient has only one diagnosis but can have two treatments. To compute frequencies of treatments, first create a new data set called TREATMENT that has either one or two observations per patient, depending on whether or not the patient had one or two treatments. Omit the cumulative statistics from the frequency tables.

PROBLEM 2

Converting Letters to Morse Code

Tools

ARRAY statement

RANK function

User-defined informat or format

Data

A line of text of your choosing

Directions

Write a SAS program that reads a line of text, converts the letters to Morse code, and prints out the code to the OUTPUT window or to your output device using FILE and PUT statements. Do this two ways:

A. Use the elements of an array to hold the Morse code values and compute which array element corresponds to a specific letter using one of the string functions.

B. Use a user-defined format or informat to provide the correspondence between the letters and the Morse code equivalents.

For those of you who are a bit rusty, the Morse code equivalents for the letters A to Z are

```
A=.-    B=-...  C=-.-.  D=-..   E=.    F=..-.  G=--.   H=....  I=..
J=.---  K=-.-   L=.-..  M=--    N=-.   O=---   P=.--.  Q=--.-  R=.-.
S=...   T=-     U=..-   V=...-  W=.--  X=-..-  Y=-.--  Z=--..
```

PROBLEM 3

Cleaning Data and Writing a Simple Report

Tools

LAG and INT functions

WHERE= data set option

FILE and PUT statements

DATA _NULL_

IN statement

Data

SAS data set CLINICAL

Directions

This project includes data cleaning and simple reporting. Write a SAS program to accomplish the following tasks.

A. Check if the value of the variable ID is missing for any observation. If so, print out the message ID is missing for the subject following, and print out the ID of the *previous* ID in the data set. If the ID that is missing is the first ID in the file, print a special message, The first ID is missing. Also check if any visit date is earlier than the date of birth. Print out an error message giving ID, DOB, and the visit date for these patients. If either the visit date or the DOB is missing, do not print an error message.

B. Search for values of SBP below 100 or above 200 and for values of DBP below 50 or above 180. Create a separate data set called BP_HI_LO with any observations that meet these criteria. Be careful not to include an observation in BP_HI_LO when the SBP or DBP is missing. Use PROC PRINT to list out these observations.

C. Prepare a report of ID, HR, SBP, and DBP for all patients who are older than 50 (as of May 1, 1996). You may use an approximate age calculation. Provide a title, and label the columns of the report as shown here.

```
Report for All Patients Older than Fifty Years Old
--------------------------------------------------
Subject  Heart   Systolic   Diastolic
         Rate     Blood       Blood
                 Pressure    Pressure
```

D. For all patients with a primary diagnosis (PRIM_DX) of 01, 02, or 04, compute frequencies for the variables GENDER, VITAMINS, and PREGNANT. Do not create a separate data set for this part.

E. Create a data set (PREG_35) containing all observations in CLINICAL for women who are pregnant and over 35 years of age (as of May 1, 1996). List the ID, AGE (as of the last birthday), and vitamin status of these women.

SECTION 4 Statistics Problems

CHAPTERS

Chapter 22 | Basic Descriptive Statistics

PROBLEMS

INTRODUCTION

The problems in this section cover topics ranging from simple descriptive statistics to more advanced repeated measures analysis of variance. You can use them to sharpen your statistical programming skills, and you can use the solutions as model programs for similar statistical problems.

You may notice that the Tools lists do not go into as much detail (such as statements and options) as those in previous chapters. The reason for this is that too much detail in the Tools list would give too many hints on how to solve the problems and ruin your fun.

These problems test your ability to generate basic descriptive statistics such as means and standard deviations; test distributions for normality; and produce frequency distributions, histograms, and two-way tables.

PROBLEM I
Producing Basic Descriptive Statistics

Tools

PROC MEANS
  BY or CLASS statements
PROC UNIVARIATE

Data

SAS data set CLINICAL

Directions

Compute the following

A. The number of non-missing observations (n), the mean, standard deviation, and standard error (all to three decimal places) for the variables HR (heart rate), SBP (systolic blood pressure), and DBP (diastolic blood pressure) for all patients.

B. The same statistics listed in A, except compute them separately for males and females.

C. The median HR, SBP, and DBP.

D. A stem-and-leaf plot for SBP. Test if the distribution is significantly different from a normal distribution (use $\alpha = .05$).

PROBLEM 2
Computing Descriptive Statistics, Broken Down by More than One Variable

Tools
PROC MEANS
    CLASS or BY statement

Data
SAS data set CLINICAL

Directions
Compute the N, mean, and standard deviation of HR, SBP, and DBP, for each level of GENDER and age group, where two age groups are defined as

```
1 = less than 65
2 = greater than or equal to 65
```

Compute age as the age at the time of the visit, dropping any fractional part of a year. Express all statistics to three decimal places.

PROBLEM 3
Generating Frequency Distributions and Histograms for Categorical Variables

Tools
PROC FREQ
PROC CHART

Data
SAS data set CLINICAL

Directions

Produce the following

A. One-way frequency tables for the variables GENDER, PRIM_DX, SEC_DX, VITAMINS, and PREGNANT.

B. Vertical bar charts for the variables GENDER and PRIM_DX.

PROBLEM 4

Generating Histograms for Numeric Variables

Tools

    PROC CHART

Data

SAS data set CLINICAL

Directions

Produce the following charts

A. Construct a histogram for the variable HR (heart rate). Let PROC CHART select the midpoints and the number of bars for the histogram.

B. Rerun part A, but specify that the midpoints for the bars should run from 40 to 100 and be spaced 10 apart.

C. Rerun part A, but specify 10 bars.

PROBLEM 5

Computing Means where There Is More than One Observation per Subject

---

Tools

    PROC MEANS

        CLASS and OUTPUT statements

Data

Raw data file CLIN_X.DTA

Directions

If you look at the contents of the CLIN_X.DTA data file you will see that there are from one to five observations for each ID. If you want to compute the mean HR, SBP, and DBP for your patients, you can first compute a mean for each ID and then take the mean of the means, or you can select a single observation for each patient (such as the first or last).

Using the CLIN_X.DTA data file, create a SAS data set and compute an overall mean for HR, SBP, and DBP using both of these methods. For the latter method, use the last visit for each patient. Compute all statistics to three decimal places.

CHAPTER 23 | Tests of Proportions

PROBLEMS

INTRODUCTION

This chapter contains problems based on testing differences in proportions. Fisher's Exact Test, chi-square tests, and McNemar's test are covered.

PROBLEM I
Computing a Chi-square and Fisher's Exact Test from Raw Data

Tools
PROC FREQ

Data
Raw data file CPR.DTA

Directions
Using the raw data in the CPR.DTA file, test if the proportion of patients surviving a cardiac arrest is related to the three independent variables ventricular fibrillation (V_FIB), patient on a respirator (RESP), and age greater than 70 (AGEGROUP). Compute both the chi-square statistic and the Fisher's exact test probability.

PROBLEM 2
Computing a Chi-square from Frequency Counts

Tools

PROC FREQ

   WEIGHT statement

Data

Data were collected on GENDER (M and F) and voting preference (candidate A and candidate B).
The data appear as follows.

```
Gender     Candidate      Count
---------------------------------
   M           A            35
   F           A            45
   M           B            70
   F           B            50
```

Directions

Using the frequency count data in the Data section, compute chi-square.

PROBLEM 3
Computing Two-way Frequencies: Chi-square and Fisher's Exact Test

Tools

PROC FREQ

Data

SAS data set CLINICAL

Directions

A. Using the SAS data set CLINICAL, create a two-way table of the variable VITAMINS by
   the variable GENDER. The table should look like the following one.

```
                        GENDER
                 Female    Male
                 ------------------
                  |    |    |     |
            No    |    |    |     |
VITAMINS         ------------------
                  |    |    |     |
            Yes   |    |    |     |
                 ------------------
```

Compute the chi-square and Fisher's exact test probability for this table. What are your conclusions if you set α at .05?

B. Write a single TABLES statement to generate two 2-way tables: the variables VITAMINS by GENDER and the variables VITAMINS by PRIM_DX.

C. Are pregnant women more likely to take vitamins than non-pregnant women based on this sample (α = .05)?

Note

Be sure to compute this table only for females.

PROBLEM 4

Computing Several Chi-square Statistics from Frequency Counts

---

Tools

> PROC FREQ
>> BY statement or three-way table
>> WEIGHT statement

Data

Frequency counts for three 2 X 2 tables

```
10  20  30  40
20  25  30  35
200 250 300 350
```

Directions

You have collected frequency counts for several 2 X 2 tables and want to enter the four counts for each table on a separate line and compute a chi-square statistic for each table. The counts are in order (A, B, C, and D; that is, top left, top right, lower left, and lower right).

Make your program general enough so that it can process any number of table requests.

PROBLEM 5
Computing a Chi-square on a 2 X 3 Table

Tools
PROC FREQ

Data
Raw data file CARS.DTA

Directions
Using the data from CARS.DTA, test if the proportion of reliability ratings below 3 are related to the size of car.

PROBLEM 6
Testing Differences in Proportions for Paired Samples: McNemar's Test (Raw Data)

Tools
PROC FREQ (Release 6.10 and above)

TABLES statement

AGREE option

Data
Opinion data as follows

SUBJECT	Opinion Before OP_BEFOR	Opinion After OP_AFTER
1	Anti	Anti
2	Anti	Pro
3	Pro	Anti
4	Pro	Anti
5	Pro	Pro
6	Anti	Pro
7	Pro	Anti
8	Pro	Anti
9	Pro	Anti
10	Pro	Anti

Directions

You have a group of subjects who had either pro- or anti-smoking opinions both before and after an educational program. Test if there is a difference in smoking attitude as a result of the educational program.

If you are running Release 6.09 or lower of base SAS software, see the solution based on creating an output data set from PROC FREQ and then computing the McNemar statistic in a subsequent DATA step, included in *The SAS Workbook Solutions*. Even if you have Release 6.10 or above, you may want to try your hand at the DATA step solution to give you some more programming practice.

Notes

1. A Release 6.10 solution is also included in *The SAS Workbook Solutions*.

2. The McNemar test on these data should actually use a correction for continuity, but go ahead and run it anyway. If you tried the DATA step solution, you can compute both the corrected and uncorrected chi-square values and the corresponding *p*-values.

PROBLEM 7

Testing Differences in Proportions for Paired Samples: McNemar's Test (Frequency Data)

Tools

PROC FREQ (Release 6.10 and above)

Data

Opinion data expressed as frequencies

Opinion Before	Opinion After	Count
Anti	Anti	70
Anti	Pro	10
Pro	Anti	40
Pro	Pro	50

Directions

Compute a McNemar's chi-square as you did in Problem 6. This time you have frequency counts instead of raw data values.

For this problem, only the Release 6.10 and above solution is presented in *The SAS Workbook Solutions*.

CHAPTER 24 | Comparing Means: Two Groups

PROBLEMS

INTRODUCTION

Problems in this chapter involve comparisons between two groups. The problems cover parametric and nonparametric tests as well as paired and unpaired tests.

PROBLEM I

Performing an Unpaired t-test (Existing SAS Data Set)

Tools

PROC TTEST

Data

SAS data set CLINICAL

Directions

Using the SAS data set CLINICAL, compare the mean HR (heart rate), SBP (systolic blood pressure), and DBP (diastolic blood pressure) between those patients who take vitamins and those who don't take vitamins.

PROBLEM 2

Performing an Unpaired t-test (Raw Data)

Tools

PROC TTEST

Data

Blood lipid data as follows

Group A			Group B		
CHOL	HDL	TRIG	CHOL	HDL	TRIG
220	45	120	155	40	130
180	60	70	120	30	170
240	75	100	112	35	160
285	50	150	126	35	120
288	55	102	133	48	80
302	70	130			

Directions

You have measured the total cholesterol (CHOL), high-density lipids (HDL), and triglycerides (TRIG) in two groups of patients. Group A was given a placebo, and group B was given a medication believed to have an effect on blood lipids.

Write a program to read these data and conduct a *t*-test on the three variables CHOL, HDL, and TRIG. For each of the variables, determine if the assumption of equal variance should be used.

PROBLEM 3

Performing an Unpaired Nonparametric Comparison (Wilcoxon Rank Sum Test)

Tools

PROC NPAR1WAY

WILCOXON option

Data

Animal weights on two different diets

```
Diet 1: 45 48 57 73 63

Diet 2: 80 72 130 65 220 200
```

Directions

Animal weights were recorded for each of two diets. Write a program to read these data and conduct a Wilcoxon rank sum test. You might want to use a Wilcoxon rank sum table to compute a more exact solution than the normal approximation values produced by PROC NPAR1WAY.

PROBLEM 4

Performing a Paired t-test

Tools

PROC MEANS

Data

Blood pressure data as follows

Subject	Systolic Blood Pressure		Diastolic Blood Pressure	
	Placebo	Drug	Placebo	Drug
1	180	160	90	80
2	220	170	110	96
3	190	140	88	78
4	182	142	108	84
5	160	154	88	86
6	190	182	88	82

Directions

An experiment was conducted in which each subject had his blood pressure measured under two different conditions: after taking a placebo for one week and after taking a blood pressure medication for one week. Using the Data in the Data section, conduct a paired *t*-test to see if there is a difference between the two conditions.

PROBLEM 5

Performing a Paired Nonparametric Comparison (Wilcoxon Signed Rank Test)

Tools

PROC UNIVARIATE

Data

The same as in Problem 4

Directions

Using the same data as Problem 4, conduct a Wilcoxon signed rank test. Compare your answer to Problem 4.

PROBLEM 6

Performing a Paired t-test with Longitudinal Data

Tools

PROC MEANS

FIRST.*variable* and LAST.*variable* temporary variable*s*

LAG function (one possible solution)

Data

Raw data file CLIN_X.DTA

Directions

Using the CLIN_X.DTA raw data file, compare the heart rate (HR) and systolic blood pressure (SBP) from the first visit to the last visit for all patients who had at least two visits. Use a paired *t*-test for the analysis. There are only four patients with two or more visits, but go ahead and run the *t*-test procedure, even though it is probably inappropriate for these data.

CHAPTER 25

Analysis of Variance

PROBLEMS

INTRODUCTION

This chapter covers a wide variety of analysis of variance problems from simple one-way balanced designs to multi-way repeated measures, unbalanced designs.

I should say a few words about terminology before letting you loose on these problems. My use of the term "repeated" is based on a common use in the medical field and described in a text, *Statistical Principles in Experimental Design, Second Edition*, by B. J. Winer (1971). I use the term "repeated" in this chapter to mean any factor where each subject is measured on every level of that factor. For example, if a runner is timed running on two different types of track surfaces, I am considering "surface" as a repeated measure factor. Other authors use the term "repeated" to refer only to factors that cannot be assigned in random order, such as time. If you use the latter meaning of "repeated", feel free to substitute your design terminology in these problems.

PROBLEM 1
Performing a One-way ANOVA (Balanced Design)

Tools
PROC ANOVA

Data
Tomato and fertilizer data as follows

Fertilizer	Tomato Weight
5-10-5	.85
5-10-5	.88
5-10-5	.87
5-10-5	.83
5-10-10	.92
5-10-10	.97
5-10-10	.86
5-10-10	.88
20-5-5	.64
20-5-5	.50
20-5-5	.48
20-5-5	.42

Directions
An experiment was conducted in which the weight of tomatoes was measured after administration of three types of fertilizer. Conduct a one-way ANOVA comparing the fertilizers. Include a request for a Student-Newman-Keuls multiple comparison test (α=.05).

PROBLEM 2
Performing a One-way ANOVA (Unbalanced Design)

Tools
PROC ANOVA

Data
Raw data file CARS.DTA

Directions
Using the data from CARS.DTA, conduct a one-way ANOVA comparing gas mileage among the three sizes of cars. Include a request for a Duncan multiple-range test conducted at α=.05 and a Scheffé test conducted at α=.10.

Hint

Remember that PROC ANOVA can be used for one-way unbalanced designs.

PROBLEM 3

Performing a Two-way ANOVA (Balanced Design) with an Interaction Plot

---

Tools

> PROC ANOVA
> PROC MEANS
> PROC PLOT
> Concatenation operator (DATA step)

Data

Activity scores on control and ADD children as follows

GROUP	DRUG	ACTIVITY
ADD	PLACEBO	90
ADD	PLACEBO	88
ADD	PLACEBO	95
CONTROL	PLACEBO	60
CONTROL	PLACEBO	62
CONTROL	PLACEBO	66
ADD	RITALIN	72
ADD	RITALIN	70
ADD	RITALIN	64
CONTROL	RITALIN	86
CONTROL	RITALIN	86
CONTROL	RITALIN	82

Directions

Two groups of children, one with attention deficit disorder (ADD) and a control group of children without ADD, were randomly given either a placebo or the drug Ritalin. A measure of activity was made on all the children with the results shown in the Data section (higher numbers indicate more activity).

A. Conduct a two-way ANOVA (GROUP by DRUG) on these data. Run a Duncan multiple-range test on any significant main effects. Draw an interaction plot like the following one.

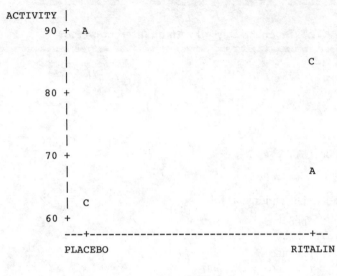

```
      Plot of ACTIVITY*DRUG.   Symbol is value of GROUP.


ACTIVITY |
      90 +  A
         |
         |                                                    C
         |
      80 +
         |
         |
         |
      70 +
         |                                                    A
         |
         |   C
      60 +
         ---+--------------------------------+--
         PLACEBO                          RITALIN


                            DRUG
```

B. Write the SAS statements to conduct a *t*-test between drugs for the ADD and control children separately. You will find a highly significant interaction term in this two-way model.

C. An alternative approach is to run a one-way ANOVA with each combination of GROUP and DRUG as levels of the independent variable. For example, the four levels would be ADD-PLACEBO, ADD-RITALIN, CONTROL-PLACEBO, and CONTROL-RITALIN. Write a DATA step that creates a new variable (call it LEVEL) that has each of these four values. Then rerun a one-way ANOVA using this new variable as the independent (CLASS) variable. Include a request for a Duncan multiple-range test.

PROBLEM 4
Performing a Two-way ANOVA (Unbalanced Design)

Tools
PROC GLM

Data
SAS data set CLINICAL

Directions

Using the SAS data set CLINICAL, conduct a two-way ANOVA on systolic blood pressure (SBP) with GENDER and VITAMINS as the independent (CLASS) variables.

PROBLEM 5
Performing a Three-way ANOVA (Balanced Design)

Tools

> PROC ANOVA
>
> DO loops in the DATA step (optional)

Data

Headache data as follows

```
Drug   Gender   Dose   Cure Time
---------------------------------
 A       M       Low       22
 A       M       High      20
 A       F       Low       18
 A       F       High      16
 B       M       Low       38
 B       M       High      34
 B       F       Low       34
 B       F       High      30
 A       M       Low       21
 A       M       High      18
 A       F       Low       17
 A       F       High      14
 B       M       Low       37
 B       M       High      33
 B       F       Low       34
 B       F       High      29
```

Directions

A drug study was conducted to measure how long it took for two different medications to cure headaches. Men and women subjects were given either a high or low dose of either drug A or drug B. The time in minutes it took for their headaches to be cured was recorded and is shown in the Data section.

Create a SAS data set using these data, and write the SAS statements to conduct a three-way ANOVA with CURETIME as the dependent variable and DRUG, GENDER, and DOSE as the independent variables.

As an interesting exercise, see if you can read the data arranged like this

```
22 20 18 16 38 34 34 30
21 18 17 14 37 33 34 29
```

The first number is the cure time for DRUG=A, GENDER=M, and DOSE=Low; the second number is the cure time for DRUG=A, GENDER=M and DOSE=High, and so on.

PROBLEM 6
Performing a Three-way ANOVA (Unbalanced Design)

Tools
PROC GLM

Data
Third and fourth grade spelling data as follows

```
                Grade 3                    Grade 4
        Phonetic      Memory    Phonetic        Memory
     ----------------------------------------------------
          35            30         45             40
Boys      37            .          48             42
          34            37         47             41
          34            29         44             39
     ----------------------------------------------------
          37            32         44             42
Girls     39            38         50             .
          37            38         49             44
          36            39         45             40
```

Directions
Boys and girls in the third and fourth grade were trained to spell in two ways. One way (we'll call it phonetic) taught the children phonetic rules; the other way (we'll call it memory) taught spelling by repetition and memorization. The children were asked to spell 50 words with the number of words spelled correctly recorded as shown in the Data section. (Notice the two missing values, making this an unbalanced design.)

Run an analysis of variance to test this factorial model. Remember that each number in the table represents a different student. Try writing your program so that you can enter the data as shown here, with the DATA step creating the appropriate GRADE, METHOD, and GENDER variables.

```
35 30 45 40
37  . 48 42
34 37 47 41
34 29 44 39
37 32 44 42
39 38 50  .
37 38 49 44
36 39 45 40
```

Hint

A couple of nested DO loops would be nice. Also remember that you can have loops such as
`DO GENDER = 'Boys ','Girls';`

PROBLEM 7

Performing a One-way ANOVA (Repeated Measures Design)

Tools

PROC ANOVA

    REPEATED statement (optional)

    CONTRAST keyword

Data

Number of problems answered correctly under different noise conditions as follows

Subject	--- Noise Level ---		
	None	Medium	High
1	20	15	8
2	10	8	4
3	35	25	23
4	9	5	2
5	28	24	20

Directions

Each of five subjects was asked to do mental arithmetic under three noise conditions (none, medium, and high). The number of problems answered correctly was recorded.

Keeping in mind that this is a repeated measures design (each subject is measured under each of the three noise conditions), run a repeated measures ANOVA. If there is a significant main effect, use an SNK multiple comparison test to detect pairwise differences. As an interesting exercise, what would be the result if you ignored the repeated aspect of this design and ran a one-way ANOVA on noise level?

Hint

You may want to rearrange the data (by rearranging the lines of data following the DATALINES statement, by writing a DATA step, or by using PROC TRANSPOSE) so that they look like this

```
Subject   Level   Number
------------------------
   1      None      20
   1      Medium    15
   1      High       8
   2      None      10
   2      Medium     8
   2      High       4
          more data observations
```

You may also want to try using the original data structure and the REPEATED statement of PROC ANOVA.

PROBLEM 8
Performing a Two-way ANOVA (Repeated Measure on One Factor)

Tools

PROC ANOVA

TEST statements specifying error terms

Data

Reaction times under different levels of alcohol consumption as follows

```
                   ----- Condition -------
Subject   Gender   Control   1 oz.   3 oz.
------------------------------------------
   1        M        .4       .9     1.2
   2        M        .6       .6      .8
   3        M        .8      1.1     1.3
   4        F        .9      1.1     1.4
   5        F       1.0      1.5     2.0
   6        F        .8      1.0     1.6
```

Directions

Male and female subjects are tested for reaction time under three different conditions: control, 1 oz. alcohol, and 3 oz. alcohol. The results are summarized in the Data section.

Create a SAS data set containing the variables SUBJECT, GENDER, COND (condition), and REACT (reaction time) with three observations per subject. Run a two-way ANOVA (GENDER by COND) with COND treated as a repeated measures factor. (You can also think of this as subjects nested within GENDER.) Run a multiple comparison test on COND to see which pairwise comparisons are significant. Use the Duncan multiple-range test to do this.

PROBLEM 9

Performing a Two-way ANOVA (Repeated Measure on Both Factors)

Tools

> PROC ANOVA
>> REPEATED statement

Data

Times to run 100 yards under different conditions as follows

	Track			
	Cinder		Rubber	
Brand of Shoe	A	B	A	B
Runner 1	11.4	11.5	10.9	10.9
2	10.8	10.7	10.2	10.0
3	10.9	11.1	10.7	10.4
4	10.4	11.2	10.5	10.7

Directions

Each of four runners was timed running 100 yards on a cinder track and on a composite rubber track, each with two different brands of shoes (Brand A and Brand B). Each runner therefore ran on two types of tracks and wore two different brands of shoes for a total of four runs. The times are listed in the Data section.

Realizing that this is a two-way design with both factors repeated, run an analysis of variance testing for the main effects and the interaction term. Try running this with *and* without the REPEATED statement of PROC ANOVA.

PROBLEM 10

Performing a Three-way ANOVA (Repeated Measure on One Factor)

Tools

PROC ANOVA

TEST statement

Data

Time to complete a puzzle by young school children as follows

		Age 3			Age 4	
Trial	1	2	3	1	2	3
	52	48	46	45	40	30
Pre-school	51	47	45	44	38	27
	53	49	47	46	41	32
	60	58	56	52	48	40
No Pre-school	59	57	55	51	47	39
	61	59	57	53	49	41

Directions

School children, ages three and four were asked to complete a simple puzzle. Some of the children attend preschool and others do not. Each child was given three tries to complete the puzzle with the time to completion recorded each time (in seconds). The results are listed in the Data section.

Test the main effects and the two- and three-way interactions. You may want to read in the data as in Problem 6. Since you want to conduct a multiple comparison test on the variable TRIAL, run a model that does not use the REPEATED statement (although this could be accomplished using CONTRAST statements).

PROBLEM 11

Performing a Three-way ANOVA (Repeated Measure on Two Factors)

Tools

PROC ANOVA

REPEATED or TEST statements

Data

The number of correctly identified license plate letters identified under several different conditions as follows

| Font | ---------------- Color Combination ---------------- | | | | | |
| | White on Blue | | Blue on White | | Black on Yellow | |
	Helv	Times	Helv	Times	Helv	Times
Policeman	21	25	22	23	18	19
	21	25	23	24	22	24
	24	22	25	20	19	21
	27	20	25	18	20	20
Lay Public	19	21	20	21	17	16
	21	21	22	22	20	20
	20	20	24	18	17	19
	24	19	25	17	20	18

Directions

An experiment was conducted to determine which combinations of colors and fonts would be most readable for car license plates by policemen and the public. Three color combinations (white on blue, blue on white, and black on yellow) were each tried with a sans serif font (Helvetica) and a serif font (Times Roman). The number of correctly identified letters or numbers was recorded after a .2 second look at each of several plates. Each policeman and each lay observer was tested on all three colors and both fonts with the results listed in the Data section.

You may want to read in these data as in Problem 6, but that is your choice. Run a three-way ANOVA (COLOR x FONT x GROUP (Police/Lay)) with both COLOR and FONT treated as repeated measures factors. The solutions both with and without the REPEATED statement are found in *The SAS Workbook Solutions*.

PROBLEM 12

Performing a Three-way ANOVA (Repeated Measures on All Factors)

Tools

PROC ANOVA

TEST statement

Data

Time on a treadmill by volunteer subjects under several conditions as follows

| | | Drug A | | | | | | Drug B | | | | |
| | | Morning | | | Night | | | Morning | | | Night | |
Trial		1	2	3	1	2	3	1	2	3	1	2	3
Subject	1	8	7	9	10	12	13	12	13	15	15	17	16
	2	9	10	11	12	13	14	15	16	17	18	19	20
	3	7	7	9	9	8	10	9	9	11	11	13	15
	4	8	9	9	8	9	9	9	10	10	10	11	12
	5	8	8	11	8	9	12	10	12	14	10	13	15

Directions

Five volunteers were asked to run on a treadmill as long as they could. They did this three times after taking each of two drugs. The treadmill test was also given either the first thing in the morning or at night. Thus, each volunteer completed 3 x 2 x 2 = 12 runs on the treadmill. The maximum time, in minutes, on the treadmill was recorded and is displayed in the Data Section.

Realizing that this is a completely repeated measures design, run the three-way design, testing for the three main effects (DRUG, TIME, and TRIAL) as well as the two- and three-way interactions.

CHAPTER 26

Parametric and Nonparametric Correlations

PROBLEMS

INTRODUCTION

A valuable step before running multiple regression models is to compute the correlations among the variables in your model. Independent variables that are strongly correlated may create problems in multiple regression models. You may want to create new variables from sets of highly correlated variables before running your regression models.

PROBLEM 1

Creating a Simple Correlation Matrix

Tools

    PROC CORR
        NOSIMPLE option
        VAR statement

Data

SAS data set CLINICAL

Directions

Generate a matrix of Pearson correlation coefficients for the variables HR (heart rate), SBP (systolic blood pressure), and DBP (diastolic blood pressure) from the SAS data set CLINICAL. Include the NOSIMPLE option to eliminate the listing of descriptive statistics that precede the correlation matrix.

PROBLEM 2
Correlating a Single Variable against a List of Variables

Tools

PROC CORR
ALPHA option
VAR and WITH statements

Data

Student quiz data as follows

The student ID is in columns 1-3 and the ten scored items are in columns 5-14. A one indicates a correct answer, and a zero indicates an incorrect answer.

```
001 1101111011
002 1111111111
003 1110101010
004 0001010001
005 1110101010
006 0101010101
007 1111111011
008 1110111011
009 0001000100
010 1111011110
```

Directions

You have test score data for some students who took a ten-question multiple choice test. For each student, you have an ID and a score (0 or 1) for each of the ten questions.

First, compute a raw score (the number of items correct) for each student. Next, compute the correlation of each of the ten questions with the raw score (this correlation is called a point-biserial correlation coefficient and is a measure of item quality). Finally, compute Cronbach's coefficient alpha for the ten questions.

Note

Since the items are dichotomous, Cronback's coefficient alpha will be equivalent to the popular Kuder-Richardson Formula 20.

Hint

The ALPHA option generates Cronbach's alpha. This option can only be used with variables listed in the VAR statement and cannot be used if there is a WITH statement present.

PROBLEM 3
Computing Spearman Rank Order Correlations

Tools

> PROC CORR
>> PEARSON, SPEARMAN, and NOSIMPLE options
>
> PROC PLOT

Data

X, Y, and Z values for several subjects

```
X     Y     Z
--------------
1     5     3
2     5     8
5     4    11
4     9    15
5    18    13
20    25    55
```

Directions

Given the values for X, Y, and Z in the Data section, compute both Pearson and Spearman correlations. Omit the descriptive statistics. Generate plots of X versus Y, X versus Z, and Y versus Z. Use the author's favorite plotting symbol o (lowercase letter o) for your plots. Compare the Pearson and Spearman coefficients and examine the scatter plots, especially for the variable pairs where the coefficients differ the most.

PROBLEM 4
Correlating Ranked Data and Comparing the Results to the Spearman Correlations

Tools

> PROC RANK
>
> PROC CORR

Data

The same as in Problem 3

Directions

Given the sample data in Problem 3, use PROC RANK to create ranks for X, Y, and Z. Generate a Pearson correlation between the ranked values and compare the results to the Spearman coefficients in Problem 3.

CHAPTER 27

Simple, Multiple, and Logistic Regression

PROBLEMS

INTRODUCTION

This chapter presents a variety of regression problems, starting with simple linear regression and ending with multiple stepwise regression and logistic regression.

PROBLEM 1

Performing Simple Linear Regression

Tools

PROC REG

PLOT statement

Data

SAS data set CLINICAL

Directions

Using the variables SBP (systolic blood pressure) and DBP (diastolic blood pressure) from the SAS data set CLINICAL, regress SBP on DBP (SBP on the y-axis, DBP on the x-axis). What is the slope and intercept of the least squares regression line? Plot the original data and the points on the regression line in one plot (use separate plotting symbols for the original data points and the predicted values) and the residuals versus DBP on another. Use the PLOT statement of PROC REG to construct these plots. Do not use an OUTPUT statement to create a data set and PROC PLOT to do the plotting.

PROBLEM 2
Plotting 95% Confidence Intervals

Tools
PROC REG

PLOT statement

Data
SAS data set CLINICAL

Directions
Using the blood pressure data from Problem 1, create a plot showing the predicted *y*-values (systolic blood pressure) and two types of 95% confidence intervals: one for individual data points, the other for the confidence limits for the mean of Y. Use a lowercase o for the predicted value, a dash (-) for the upper and lower limits of the 95% confidence interval for individual points, and an equal sign (=) for the upper and lower 95% confidence interval for the mean of Y.

PROBLEM 3
Using the Simple Regression Equation to Predict Values

Tools
PROC REG

MODEL statement

P, R, CLI, and CLM options

Data
Values of X and Y as follows

```
    X       Y
  --------
    1       4
    2       7
    5      12
    7      15
```

Directions
Using the values from the Data section, generate a least squares regression line and predict the y-value for x-values of 10 and 20. Also create printed output showing the predicted value and the 95% confidence limits (both types) for all values of DBP (diastolic blood pressure).

Hint

Use the MODEL statement options P, R, CLI, and CLM to print the requested values. Include *x*-values of 10 and 20 (with missing values for Y) in your data set to compute predicted *y*-values.

PROBLEM 4
Performing Multiple Regression (Fixed Model)

Tools
    PROC REG

Data

Raw data file CARS.DTA

Directions

Using the raw data file CARS.DTA, predict gas mileage (MILEAGE) based on car SIZE and reliability (RELIABLE).

A. Use the values 1, 2, and 3 to represent SMALL, COMPACT, and MID-SIZED cars, respectively.

B. Create two dummy variables to specify the three car sizes.

PROBLEM 5
Performing Multiple Regression Using Several Selection Methods

Tools
    PROC REG
        MODEL statement
            SELECTION= option

Data
SAS data set CLINICAL

Directions

Using the SAS data set CLINICAL, generate a multiple regression equation that predicts systolic blood pressure (SBP) using gender, age, heart rate (HR), and diastolic blood pressure (DBP) as predictor variables. First, run a model with all of these variables included. Next, run the STEPWISE procedure to fit a model. Finally, use the RSQUARE selection method to run all one-, two-, three-, and four-variable models.

Note that you need to compute AGE in a DATA step and create a dummy variable based on GENDER (GENDER is stored as a character variable with values of M, and F). There are really too few observations to include this many variables in a regression, but solve the problem for practice.

PROBLEM 6
Performing Logistic Regression

Tools

PROC LOGISTIC
>   DESCENDING option
>   MODEL statement
>>   SELECTION=, CTABLE, and RL options

Data

Raw data file CPR.DTA

Directions

Create a SAS data set from the raw data file CPR.DTA. Run a forward stepwise logistic regression with SURVIVE (survival) as the dependent variable and V_FIB (is the patient in ventricular fibrillation?), RESP (was the patient on a respirator prior to the cardiac arrest?), and AGEGROUP (is age greater than 70?) as the independent variables.

Note that for the dependent variable, a value of 1 (yes) represents survival; and a value of 0 (no) represents no survival (death). Your equation should predict the odds ratios for survival. The default for PROC LOGISTIC is to predict the odds ratio for the lower value of the dependent variable (in this case a 0). Thus, you need to create a new variable with the lower value being survival or, more simply, use the DESCENDING option (as suggested in the Tools list). For the variables V_FIB and RESP, a 0 indicates that the patient did not have this condition and a 1 indicates that he or she did. For the variable AGEGROUP, a value of 1 indicates the patient is older than 70; a 0 indicates he or she is 70 or younger.

Include in your output, a classification table and the 95% confidence limits on the odds ratios.

CHAPTER 28 | Random Assignment and Random Selection of Subjects

PROBLEMS

INTRODUCTION

This chapter includes problems on randomly assigning subjects to groups and random selection of samples from larger data sets.

PROBLEM 1

Assigning Subjects into Two Groups

Tools

RANUNI function

PROC RANK

GROUPS= option

Data

Generated in a DATA step

Directions

You want to assign each of 50 subjects to either group A or group B by either

A. Using a randomly generated value to assign subjects to either group A or group B with an equal probability that the subject will be assigned to either A or B. The number of subjects assigned to the groups may not be equal.

B. Using a combination of random numbers and PROC RANK (with the GROUPS=2 option) to assign subjects randomly to either group A or group B with the requirement that there be an equal number of subjects (25) in the two groups.

For both methods, provide a listing of the subjects and their group assignment and a count of the number of subjects in each of the two groups.

Note

Use a fixed seed for the random number function rather than the clock seed. For example, RANUNI(1357).

PROBLEM 2

Assigning Subjects into Three Groups

Tools

RANUNI function

PROC RANK

GROUPS= option

Data

Generated in a DATA step

Directions

Repeat parts A and B from Problem 1, but this time you want a total of 30 subjects assigned to either group A, B, or C. For part B, you will have ten subjects in each of the three groups.

PROBLEM 3

Assigning Subjects into Groups, Balanced in Blocks

Tools

RANUNI function

PROC RANK

GROUPS= option

Nested DO loops

Data

Generated in a DATA step

Directions

This problem is similar to Problem 1 (part B) except that you want to avoid long runs of either group A or group B assignments. You want to assign 50 subjects to either group A or group B, and you want an equal number of subjects assigned to A and B every ten subjects. That is, for each block of ten subjects, there will be five A's and five B's.

PROBLEM 4

Taking a Random Subset of Subjects

Tools

RANUNI function

Data

SAS data set BIG created by running the following program

```
DATA BIG;
   DO SUBJECT = 1 TO 100;
       X = INT (RANUNI(0)*100 + 1);
       OUTPUT;
   END;
RUN;
```

Directions

You have a data set BIG with 100 observations and you want a 5% random sample. Call the 5% random sample data set SMALL.

A. Solve this problem with an approximate solution using a test for the value of a random variable.

B. Write a program what will always generate a sample of five observations at random from data set BIG.

CHAPTER 29

PROBLEMS

INTRODUCTION

The problems in this chapter are longer and, perhaps, more difficult than those in the earlier chapters. They are more typical of real world problems and may be a little more vague than previous problems. If you are a student in a research course or a researcher wanting to practice your statistical programming skills, they should be good practice.

PROBLEM 1

Creating a SAS Data Set Complete with Formats and Labels, Descriptive Statistics, Simple Hypothesis Tests, Correlations, and Multiple Regression

Tools

PROC PRINT
PROC UNIVARIATE
PROC FREQ
PROC TTEST
PROC NPAR1WAY
PROC CORR
PROC GLM

Data

All sections of this problem use the SAS data set CLINICAL

Directions

A. Create a new data set from CLINICAL which includes the subject's approximate age in years as of the last clinic visit. Truncate this value (i.e., compute age as of the last birthday at the time of the visit).

B. Provide a listing of this data set. Use the variable labels as column headings. Remember that this data set already has labels and formats associated with the variables. If you made the original CLINICAL data set permanent, remember to let the program know where to find the user-defined formats.

C. Compute descriptive statistics, including a test for normality and stem-and-leaf plots, for the variables HR, SBP, DBP, and AGE.

D. Generate the following tables:

   1. One-way frequencies for GENDER, PRIM_DX, SEC_DX, and VITAMINS.

   2. Crosstab of GENDER by VITAMINS including a Fisher's exact test.

E. Generate frequencies for the variable PREGNANT. Do this for females only since this variable is set to 0 (no) for male patients.

F. Investigate the relationship between vitamin use and pregnancy by comparing the proportion of pregnant and non-pregnant females using vitamins, again being sure this is computed only for females.

G. Compute a *t*-test with GENDER as the independent variable and HR, SBP, DBP, and AGE as dependent variables. Indicate which *t*- and *p*-value to use for each test, based on the assumption of homogeneity of variance being met or not.

H. Repeat the comparisons in part G using a nonparametric test (Wilcoxon rank sum test) instead of a *t*-test.

I. Generate a correlation matrix among the variables HR, SBP, DBP, and AGE. Omit simple statistics and compute both Spearman and Pearson correlations.

J. In preparing to run an analysis of covariance with SBP and DBP as dependent variables, GENDER as the independent variable, and AGE as a covariate, test if the assumption of homogeneity of slope is violated. That is, test if the slope of AGE by SBP and AGE by DBP is significantly different ($p < .05$) for males versus females.

K. For any dependent variables in part J where the assumption of homogeneity of slope is valid, run an analysis of covariance and compute the adjusted means.

L. Run a multiple regression with SBP as the dependent variable and GENDER, DBP, and AGE as predictor (independent) variables. Use a forward stepwise selection method. Since GENDER is a character variable with values of M and F, create a new variable (SEX) which is numeric and has a value of 0 for males and 1 for females.

M. Compute frequencies for all diagnoses, treating primary and secondary diagnoses equally. That is, if one patient has code 01 as a primary diagnosis and another patient has code 01 as a secondary diagnosis, you would count two people as having diagnosis 01. To accomplish this task, create a new data set called DX_FREQ which has as many observations as there are diagnosis codes in the original data set (PRIM_DX codes plus SEC_DX). If a patient has a primary diagnosis and a secondary diagnosis, that patient will contribute two observations to DX_FREQ.

PROBLEM 2
Computing a Two-way ANOVA with a Significant Interaction Term

Tools
PROC ANOVA
PROC MEANS
   OUTPUT statement
Concatenation operator
PROC TTEST
PROC PLOT

Data
Values of GROUP, GENDER, and X as follows

GROUP	GENDER	X
A	M	5
A	M	6
A	M	7
A	F	11
A	F	13
A	F	14
B	M	15
B	M	10
B	M	11
B	F	4
B	F	6
B	F	7

Directions

A. Given the data described, conduct a two-way ANOVA for the variable X with GROUP and GENDER as independent variables. You will find that the GROUP*GENDER term is significant (and the main effects are not).

B. Use PROC MEANS to create an output data set with the mean value of X for each combination of GROUP and GENDER.

C. Use this data set to produce an interaction plot as shown here.

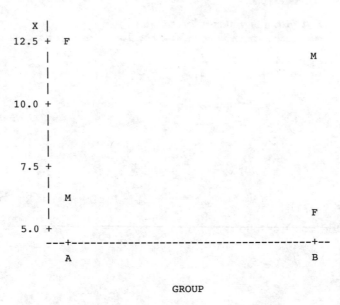

```
        Plot of X*GROUP.  Symbol is value of GENDER.


      X |
   12.5 +   F
        |                                          M
        |
        |
   10.0 +
        |
        |
        |
    7.5 +
        |
        |   M
        |                                          F
    5.0 +
        ---+-----------------------------------+--
           A                                   B


                          GROUP
```

D. Conduct a *t*-test with GROUP as the independent variable for each level of GENDER.

E. Create a data set which contains a new variable (CATEGORY) which has values of A–M, A–F, B–M, and B–F (that is, a value reflecting both the GROUP and GENDER). Using this new variable, conduct a one-way ANOVA with X as the dependent variable and CATEGORY as the independent variable. Follow this ANOVA with a Student-Newman-Keuls multiple comparison test.

PROBLEM 3

Performing an Unpaired t-test Using a Variety of Input Data Arrangements

Tools

PROC TTEST

A variety of input methods and DATA step programming

Data

Respiration data as follows

```
Subject    Group    Respiration Rate (RESP)
-----------------------------------------------

   1         A            16
   2         A            20
   3         A            18
   4         B            24
   5         B            22
   6         B            28
   7         B            18
```

Directions

Subjects were assigned to either group A or group B, and the number of breaths per minute (respirations) was recorded for each subject.

For each of the sections that follow, the data values are arranged differently. Write the SAS statements necessary to create a SAS data set called BREATH containing the variables SUBJECT, GROUP, and RESP. Follow this with a request for an unpaired *t*-test comparing the mean respiration rates for groups A and B.

A. The data arrangement for this part is

```
A 16
A 20
A 18
B 24
B 22
B 28
B 18
```

Notice that there is no subject number in the data, and you want a SUBJECT variable in the data set.

B. Similar to part A except the data values are all on one line.

```
A 16   A 20   A 18   B 24   B 22   B 28   B 18
```

C. The data are arranged as follows

```
A 16 20 18
B 24 22 28 18
```

You are told that there are three values for group A and four values for group B, but this number is not to be placed in the data. You need to program the number of scores to read for each group in the DATA step.

D. The data are arranged as follows

```
16 20 18 24 22 28 18
```

You are told that the first three numbers are for group A and the next four numbers are for group B. This time the value of GROUP and the number of scores to read for each group must be programmed in the DATA step.

E. The data are arranged as follows

```
3 16 20 18 4 24 22 28 18
```

The number of subjects is entered, followed by the respiration values. You are told that the first set of numbers are from group A and the second set are from group B.

F. The data are arranged as follows

```
A 16 B 24 22 A 20 18 B 28 18
```

That is, a group letter is followed by one or more scores. Have the program read each data value and decide if it is a group letter or a score. Write the program in a general way such that it will work for any arrangement of groups and scores. For example, the program should be able to read the following data line without making any changes

```
A 16 20 B 24 B 22 28 18 A 18
```

It is not necessary for the subject number to match the other data sets. Just make sure that each observation has a sequential subject number.

G. The data are arranged as follows

```
A 3 16 20 18
B 4 24 22 28 18
```

The number of subjects in each group follows the group code, followed by all the data values.

PROBLEM 4

*Creating New Variables, Regrouping Data, Producing Descriptive Statistics,
and Performing Significance Tests on Means and Proportions*

Tools

Date literal

ROUND and LOG functions

PROC FREQ

PROC UNIVARIATE

WHERE statement

PROC TTEST

PROC NPAR1WAY

PROC ANOVA

Data

SAS data set CLINICAL

Directions

A. Create a new data set called HOSPITAL that contains the following new variables:

```
AGE        Age as of 1/1/96 rounded to the nearest year
AGE_GRP    Where ages 0-40 = 1; 41-65 = 2; >65 = 3
LOG_SBP    Natural (base e) LOG of Systolic Blood Pressure (SBP)
```

B. Compute Fisher's exact test to determine if the proportion of males is equal for the people who take vitamins compared to people who do not take vitamins.

C. Compute the mean and standard deviation of SBP and LOG_SBP for each gender. Test if the means are significantly different using a parametric and a nonparametric test.

D. Find the median HR for females (GENDER=F).

E. Test if the means for SBP and LOG_SBP are different as a function of AGE_GRP (as defined in part A above). Conduct a Duncan multiple comparison test.

PROBLEM 5
Working with Paired Data

Tools

PROC FREQ

PROC NPAR1WAY

RENAME= data set option

PROC SORT

MERGE statement

PROC UNIVARIATE

Data

Case-control study data as follows

SUBJ_ID	MATCH_ID	GROUP	A	B	C	X
1	11	CASE	1	0	1	23
2	.	CASE	1	1	1	33
3	12	CASE	1	1	0	28
4	14	CASE	1	1	1	29
5	18	CASE	0	1	1	33
6	23	CASE	1	0	0	77
11	1	CONT	0	0	0	41
12	3	CONT	1	0	0	29
13	.	CONT	0	1	1	55
14	4	CONT	0	0	0	56
18	5	CONT	0	0	0	32

Directions

A researcher conducted a case-control study where each case was matched against a single control, based on gender and age (plus or minus five years). The collected data is displayed in the Data section.

A. Start out by creating a data set called UNPAIRED from the raw data and conducting an unpaired analysis using all available data. Compute a Fisher's exact test for the variables A, B, and C versus GROUP and a Wilcoxon rank sum test for the variable X, with GROUP as the independent variable.

B. Next, select all cases and controls who are paired and construct a data set called PAIRED, where the cases and their matched controls are in the same observation. For example, the first few observations in this new data set would be

```
SUBJ_ID  CASE_A CASE_B CASE_C CONT_A CONT_B CONT_C CASE_X CONT_X
------------------------------------------------------------------
   1        1      0      1      0      0      0      23     41
   3        1      1      0      1      0      0      28     29
                         more observations
```

One way to accomplish this goal is to place all case data in one data set and all control data in another, eliminating all subjects where the MATCH_ID variable is missing. You can then rename the MATCH_ID variable in one of the data sets to SUBJ_ID, rename the remaining variables in both data sets (A becomes CASE_A in the case data set, and so on), sort both data sets by SUBJ_ID, and then merge the two data sets by SUBJ_ID, being sure to keep only subjects who form a pair.

C. Compute a McNemar chi-square for the variables that were originally called A, B, and C and conduct a Wilcoxon signed rank test for the variable X with GROUP as the independent variable.

Note

Not all cases and controls are paired.

SECTION 5 | SAS® Puzzles to Test Your Skills

CHAPTERS

Chapter 30   SAS® Puzzles

This chapter contains some interesting puzzles that are fun to try and give you some insight into the internal workings of the SAS language. Unlike the other chapters, this chapter does not contain Problem headings or Tools lists.

Most of the problems center around understanding details of the DATA step. You can check your answer on almost all the problems by running the programs and checking the results. You may need to include some PUT statements in the DATA step or run the PRINT procedure following the DATA step to check your answer. Some of the problems involve writing a few lines of SAS code. For these, you will need to check *The SAS Workbook Solutions* (or drive a colleague crazy) if you get stuck.

PROBLEM 1

After running the following program:

```
DATA PUZZLE1;
   DO I = 1 TO 6;
      INPUT X @@;
      SUBJECT = SUBJECT + 1;
   END;
DATALINES;
1 2 3
4 5 6
;
```

A. What is the value of I in observation 1?

B. How many observations are in the data set PUZZLE1?

C. What is the value of SUBJECT in the last observation?

PROBLEM 2

In the following program:

```
DATA PUZZLE2;
   DO I = 1 TO 5;
      INPUT X;
      COUNTER = _N_;
      OUTPUT;
   END;
```

```
      DROP I;
DATALINES;
1
2
3
;
```

What is the value of COUNTER for each observation?

PROBLEM 3

In the following program:

```
DATA PUZZLE3;
   INPUT X @@;
   IF X GE 5 THEN Y = LAG(X);
DATALINES;
1 8 2 10 15
;
```

What are the values of Y for each of the five observations?

PROBLEM 4

In the following program:

```
DATA PUZZLE4;
   DO I = 1 TO 5;
      I + 1;
      OUTPUT;
   END;
RUN;
```

What are the values of I for each of the observations, and how many observations are there?

PROBLEM 5

In the following program:

```
DATA PUZZLE5;
   INPUT X @@;
   IF X = 1 THEN X = 5;
   IF X = 2 THEN X = 4;
   IF X = 4 THEN X = 2;
   IF X = 5 THEN X = 1;
DATALINES;
1 3 5
;
```

What is the value of X in each of the three observations?

PROBLEM 6

In the following program:

```
DATA PUZZLE6;
   INPUT A B @@;
DATALINES;
1 1  1 2  1 3  2 1  2 2  2 3  3 1  3 2  3 3
;
PROC SORT DATA=PUZZLE6;
   BY A B;
RUN;

DATA P6;
   SET PUZZLE6;
      BY A B;
   FIRST_A = FIRST.A;
   FIRST_B = FIRST.B;
   LAST_A  = LAST.A;
   LAST_B  = LAST.B;
RUN;
```

What are the values of FIRST_A, FIRST_B, LAST_A, and LAST_B for each of the nine observations?

PROBLEM 7

In the following program:

```
DATA PUZZLE7;
   RETAIN X (9);
   INPUT X @@;
DATALINES;
1 . 2 . 3
;
```

What are the values of X in each of the five observations?

PROBLEM 8

After running the following program:

```
DATA PUZZLE8;
   INPUT X Y @;
DATALINES;
1 2 3 4 5 6 7 8
;
```

How many observations are there in data set PUZZLE8?

PROBLEM 9

You have a SAS data set called CLIFTON that contains GENDER (M or F) and AGE (rounded to the nearest year). You want to compute a new variable.

```
DATA PUZZLE9;
   SET CLIFTON;
   IF GENDER = 'M' THEN NEWVAR = AGE + 20;
   ELSE IF GENDER = 'F' THEN NEWVAR = AGE + 30;
RUN;
```

Can you rewrite this program so that NEWVAR is computed in one SAS statement?

PROBLEM 10

You are given lines of text (all less than or equal to 80 bytes) consisting of words in upper- and lowercase letters. There is at least one upper- or lowercase letter on each text line. There may be punctuation in a line (period, comma, question mark, or exclamation mark). Write a compact DATA step that counts the number of letters in each line and does not count spaces or punctuation.

Sample data to test your program

```
This is a test, this is only a TEST!!!    (count = 26)
aaa bbb    ...,,,xxx                       (count = 9)
```

Can you compute this number in one statement?

PROBLEM 11

In the program below:

```
DATA CHAR;
      LENGTH A $ 1 C $ 10;
      INPUT A $ B $ C $;
      D = REPEAT(A,20);
      E = SUBSTR(C,3,2);
      F = A || B || C;
   DATALINES;
   X YY CCCCC
   ;
```

What are the lengths of the variables A, B, C, D, E, and F?

PROBLEM 12

In the following program:

```
DATA TEST;
      DO I = 1 TO 3;
         INPUT X @@;
         N = _N_;
         OUTPUT;
      END;
   DATALINES;
   1 2 3 4 5 6
   7 8 9 10 11 12
   ;
```

What is the value of N in the last observation?

PROBLEM 13

You have a group variable with values of A, B, or C.

You want to compute a new variable TAX according to the following rule

```
For group A: TAX = .15 * INCOME
For group B: TAX = .27 * INCOME
For group C: TAX = .35 * INCOME
```

Assuming you have a data set with the variables GROUP and INCOME, write a *single* DATA step statement that will compute TAX.

PROBLEM 14

After running the following program:

```
DATA PUZZLE14;
   X = 3;
   IF X = 1 OR 2 THEN LOGIC = 'TRUE ';
   ELSE                LOGIC = 'FALSE';
RUN;
```

What is the value of LOGIC?

PROBLEM 15

You have a dichotomous character variable SMOKE with values of Y or N (assume there are no invalid or missing data). You want to create a numeric variable X_SMOKE with values of 1 or 0, corresponding to the values Y and N. Two ways to do this are

```
IF SMOKE = 'Y' THEN X_SMOKE = '1';
ELSE X_SMOKE = '0';
```

```
                or
```

```
X_SMOKE = INPUT (TRANSLATE(SMOKE,'10','YN'),1.);
```

Can you compute X_SMOKE using one statement without using any functions?

SECTION 6

APPENDIX

Appendix

File Descriptions and Data Program to Create SAS® Data Set CLINICAL

A number of raw data files and SAS data sets are used throughout this workbook. This appendix contains a description of the raw data files, a listing of the actual data files, and a program for creating a SAS data set called CLINICAL from raw data file CLINICAL.DTA. All the programs and solutions in this workbook assume that the raw data files and the permanent SAS data sets are to be stored in a subdirectory called C:\WORKBOOK. Make the appropriate adjustments if you are using another subdirectory or if you are running SAS software in a different operating environment.

You can download the data files and the program to create the SAS data set CLINICAL using the instructions located on the inside back cover of this book. If you don't have a modem, you may want to create the raw data files by typing in the data listed in the appendix. You can also enter the program CLINICAL.SAS and run it.

Data files are listed alphabetically by name.

BASKET.DTA Data File Description

Variable	Description	Starting Column	Length	Type
ID	Employee ID	1	3	Char
GENDER	Gender	5	1	Char (M or F)
HEIGHT	Height in inches	7	2	Numeric
DATE	Date of game	10	8	MM/DD/YY
POINTS	Number of points	19	2	Numeric

Listing of Raw Data from BASKET.DTA

```
          1         2
1234567890123456789 0
--------------------
001 M 72 12/01/95 10
001 M 72 12/03/95 12
001 M 72 12/10/95  8
002 F 68 10/21/95 14
003 M 74 12/12/95 20
003 M 74 12/16/95 22
004 M 74 11/12/95  6
004 M 74 11/15/95  8
005 F 67 12/12/95 10
```

```
005 F 67 12/15/95 18
006 M 69 10/30/95  2
006 M 69 11/04/95  6
006 M 69 11/06/95  8
007 M 69 11/11/95  9
007 M 69 11/16/95  7
```

BASKETBA.DTA Data File Description

```
                              Starting
Variable        Description   Column   Length   Type
------------------------------------------------------------
  ID            Employee ID      1        3     Char
  GENDER        Gender           5        1     Char (M or F)
  HEIGHT        Height in inches 7        2     Numeric
  DATE          Date of game    10        8     MM/DD/YY
  POINTS        Number of points 19       2     Numeric
```

Note

The file BASKETBA.DTA is the same as the file BASKET.DTA except that GENDER and HEIGHT are entered in only the first record for each player in the BASKETBA.DTA file, and GENDER and HEIGHT are missing for some players.

Listing of Raw Data from BASKETBA.DTA

```
          1         2
12345678901234567890
--------------------
001 M 72 12/01/95 10
001      12/03/95 12
001      12/10/95  8
002 F 68 10/21/95 14
003 M 74 12/12/95 20
003      12/16/95 22
004      11/12/95  6
004      11/15/95  8
005 F 67 12/12/95 10
005      12/15/95 18
006 M 69 10/30/95  2
006      11/04/95  6
006      11/06/95  8
007      11/11/95  9
007      11/16/95  7
```

CARS.DTA Data File Description

Variable	Description	Starting Column	Length	Type
SIZE	Car Size	1	9	Char
MANUFACT	Manufacturer	11	9	Char
MODEL	Model	22	9	Char
MILEAGE	Gas Mileage	38	2	Numeric
RELIABLE	Reliability	50	1	Numeric

Listing of Raw Data from CARS.DTA

```
          1         2         3         4         5
1234567890123456789012345678901234567890123456789 0
-----------------------------------------------------
SMALL     CHEVROLET GEO PRIZM      33          5
SMALL     HONDA     CIVIC          29          5
SMALL     TOYOTA    COROLLA        30          5
SMALL     FORD      ESCORT         27          3
SMALL     DODGE     COLT           34
COMPACT   FORD      TEMPO          24          1
COMPACT   CHRYSLER  LE BARON       23          3
COMPACT   BUICK     SKYLARK        21          3
COMPACT   PLYMOUTH  ACCLAIM        24          3
COMPACT   CHEVROLET CORSICA        25          2
COMPACT   PONTIAC   SUNBIRD        24          1
MID-SIZED TOYOTA    CAMRY          24          5
MID-SIZED HONDA     ACCORD         26          5
MID-SIZED FORD      TAURUS         20          3
```

CLIN_X.DTA Data File Description

Note

1. Multiple observations per patient

2. Not sorted by ID or visit date

3. Contains some short records (not padded with blanks)

Variable	Description	Starting Column	Length	Format	Codes
ID	Patient ID	1	3	Char	
VISIT	Date of Visit	4	6	MMDDYY	
DX	Diagnosis	10	2	Char	(see list)
HR	Heart Rate	12	3	Numeric	
SBP	Systolic Blood Pressure	15	3	Numeric	
DBP	Diastolic Blood Pressure	18	3	Numeric	
RX_1	Treatment 1	21	1	Char	(see list)
RX_2	Treatment 2	22	1	Char	(see list)

DX Codes:

01	Cold
02	Flu
03	Fracture
04	Routine Physical
05	Heart Problem
06	Lung Disorder
07	Abdominal Pain
08	Laceration
09	URI
10	Lyme Disease
11	Ear Ache

RX Codes:

1	Immunization
2	Casting
3	Beta Blocker
4	ACE Inhibitor
5	Antihistamine
6	Ibuprofen
7	Aspirin
8	Antibiotic

Listing of Raw Data from CLIN_X.DTA

```
          1         2         3
1234567890123456789012345678890
------------------------------
7770901941108809806468
0450518940408618009 2
0330105940908418280788
0451021950508821012034
0330909950206812000706
0331010950707212200748
0451031950508418010234
0091231950308813400882
0330518940108812800786
1770606950405812000 74
0451221950607815000808
0090909950707812800 82
0090701950805812800844
```

```
177081895100821300808G
445091995030881440882G
777091295070861000G2
0091015950106G1220825?
078110195050901901l073
033101095l00581200708
```

CLINICAL.DTA Data File Description

Variable	Description	Starting Column	Length	Format	Codes
ID	Subject ID	1	3	Char	
GENDER	Gender	4	1	Char	M,F
DOB	Date of Birth	5	6	MMDDYY	
VISIT	Visit Date	11	6	MMDDYY	
PRIM_DX	Primary DX Code	17	2	Char	(see list)
SEC_DX	Secondary DX Code	19	2	Char	"
HR	Heart Rate	21	3	Numeric	
SBP	Systolic Blood Pres.	24	3	Numeric	
DBP	Diastolic Blood Pres.	27	3	Numeric	
VITAMINS	Pt. Taking Vitamins?	30	1	Char	1=Yes, 0=No
PREGNANT	Is PT Pregnant?	31	1	Char	1=Yes, 0=No

DX Codes:

01	Cold	07	Abdominal Pain
02	Flu	08	Laceration
03	Fracture	09	Immunization
04	Routine Physical	10	Lyme Disease
05	Heart Problem	11	Ear Ache
06	Lung Disorder		

Listing of Raw Data from CLINICAL.DTA

```
         1         2         3         4
12345678901234567890123456789012345678901234567890
------------------------------------------
123M10214605159501050621360761 0
278F11015505159504  06810406400
444F07086505169501  07812806211
756M12256206119507090661500960 0
811F03047506019505060881660740 0
193F10105908159504  07011206811
   M10159502159604  08009805410
978M06289407029504090880980621 0
586M12040905189505060861620961 0
919F09069306209511  09205805010
529M07135008099510  05811407600
324F01011075119506  08620010010
012F10090876019503080901840980 0
812M10116710109508  06613408210
338M07289007129511  08210607010
959F12156511119507090881760981 0
007F04196402069504  07410606411
291M08097506039501110681320860 0
984F12237905159502  07409606201
669M02287707079509  06214009000
999F01019502019401  08018810200
229F06188009189509  07410406010
885M09108510159511109088114084 00
178M03049107169501090881020680 0
   F01019001069605060701200800 0
966F04059108169501090920540361 0
782M06071005189505060882201800 0
374M05068807229504  08312007000
285F06077009119511  08416009600
884M07121609119505  07819014000
258M08098211189504  07214409800
733F09097803049507020741200701 1
449M10103110189501            10
941F10107010199503040881901100 1
```

Program to Create the SAS Data Set
CLINICAL

```
*-------------------------------------------------------------------*
| Program Name: CLINICAL.SAS in subdirectory C:\WORKBOOK            |
| Purpose: To Create a Permanent SAS data set called CLINICAL from  |
|          the raw data file CLINICAL.DTA along with permanent      |
|          formats.  Both the SAS data set and permanent formats are|
|          to be stored in the subdirectory C:\WORKBOOK             |
*-------------------------------------------------------------------* ;

LIBNAME WORKBOOK 'C:\WORKBOOK';

OPTIONS PAGENO=1 NOCENTER FMTSEARCH=(WORKBOOK);

FILENAME CLIN 'C:\WORKBOOK\CLINICAL.DTA';

PROC FORMAT LIBRARY=WORKBOOK;
   VALUE $GENDER 'M' = 'Male'
                 'F' = 'Female';
   VALUE $DXCODES '01' = 'Cold'
                  '02' = 'Flu'
                  '03' = 'Fracture'
                  '04' = 'Routine Physical'
                  '05' = 'Heart Problem'
                  '06' = 'Lung Disorder'
                  '07' = 'Abdominal Pain'
                  '08' = 'Laceration'
                  '09' = 'Immunization'
                  '10' = 'Lyme disease'
                  '11' = 'Ear Ache';
   VALUE $YESNO '0' = 'No'
                '1' = 'Yes';
RUN;
```

```
DATA WORKBOOK.CLINICAL;
   INFILE CLIN;
   INPUT   @1   ID        $3.
           @4   GENDER    $1.
           @5   DOB       MMDDYY6.
           @11  VISIT     MMDDYY6.
           @17  PRIM_DX   $2.
           @19  SEC_DX    $2.
           @21  HR        3.
           @24  SBP       3.
           @27  DBP       3.
           @30  VITAMINS  $1.
           @31  PREGNANT  $1.;

   LABEL   ID        = 'Pt. Number'
           GENDER    = 'Gender'
           DOB       = 'Date of Birth'
           VISIT     = 'Visit Date'
           PRIM_DX   = 'Primary DX'
           SEC_DX    = 'Secondary DX'
           HR        = 'Heart Rate'
           SBP       = 'Systolic Blood Pressure'
           DBP       = 'Diastolic Blood Pressure'
           VITAMINS = 'Pt. Taking Vitamins?'
           PREGNANT = 'Is Pt. Pregnant?';

   FORMAT PRIM_DX SEC_DX $DXCODES.
          DOB VISIT MMDDYY8.
          GENDER $GENDER.
          VITAMINS PREGNANT $YESNO.;

RUN;
```

CPR.DTA Data File Description

Variable	Description	Starting Column	Length	Format	Codes
SUBJECT	Subject number	1	3	Numeric	
V_FIB	Ventricular Fibrillation	4	1	Numeric	1=Yes, 0=No
RESP	Pt on Respirator?	5	1	Numeric	1=Yes, 0=No
AGEGROUP	Age greater than 70?	6	1	Numeric	1=Yes, 0=No
SURVIVE	Did patient Survive?	7	1	Numeric	1=Yes, 0=No

Listing of Raw Data from File CPR.DTA

```
          1
1234567890
----------
0011001
0021111
0031110
0040010
0050010
0060110
0070011
0081001
0090000
0101011
0110000
0120101
0130100
0141111
0150101
0161001
0170011
0180010
0190110
0201011
0210110
0220010
0231110
0240001
0251011
0261110
0270110
0280110
0291100
0300100
0310001
0320010
0330001
0340100
0350010
0360001
```

DEMOG1.DTA and DEMOG2.DTA Data File Descriptions

Variable	Description	Starting Column	Length	Type	Codes
ID	Subject ID	1	3	Char	
DOB	Date of Birth	4	6	MMDDYY	
GENDER	Gender	10	1	Char	M=Male, F=Female
STATE	State of Residence	11	2	Char	
EMPLOYED	Employed?	13	1	Char	1=Yes, 0=No

Listing of Raw Data from DEMOG1.DTA

```
          1         2         3         4         5         6
1234567890123456789012345678901234567890123456789012345678901234567890
----------------------------------------------------------------
178102146MNJ1
982110166FNY0
723030452MNJ1
258101074FNY1
139122550FNJ0
145010444MNY1
```

Listing of Raw Data from DEMOG2.DTA

```
          1         2         3         4         5         6
1234567890123456789012345678901234567890123456789012345678901234567890
----------------------------------------------------------------
559110168FNY0
714010244MNH0
934052890FNJ0
569112850FNY1
```

DIALYSIS.DTA Data File Description

Variable	Description	Starting Column	Length	Type	Codes
ID	Subject ID	1	3	Char	
GENDER	Gender	4	1	Char	M=Male, F=Female
DOB	Date of Birth	5	8	MM/DD/YY	
VISIT	Visit Number	13	1	Numeric	
HR	Heart Rate	14	3	Numeric	
SBP	Systolic Blood Pressure	17	3	Numeric	
DBP	Diastolic Blood Pressure	20	3	Numeric	

Listing of Raw Data from DIALYSIS.DTA

```
          1         2         3
1234567890123456789012345678 90
------------------------------
001M10/21/461080140080
001       2082142084
001       3078138078
002F11/17/221066120070
003F04/04/181084150090
003       2088152102
004M12/21/101072120074
004       2070122076
004       3078128078
005F08/02/311092180110
006       1076180112
006       2080178090
```

Index

Call your local SAS office to order these books from Books by Users Press

Web Development with SAS® by Example
by **Frederick Pratter** . . . . Order No. A58694

Your Guide to Survey Research Using the
SAS® System
by **Archer Gravely** . . . . Order No. A55688

JMP® Books

JMP® for Basic Univariate and Multivariate Statistics: A
Step-by-Step Guide
by **Ann Lehman, Norm O'Rourke, Larry Hatcher,**
and **Edward Stepanski** . . . . Order No. A59814

JMP® Start Statistics, Third Edition
by **John Sall, Ann Lehman,**
and **Lee Creighton** . . . . Order No. A58166

Regression Using JMP®
by **Rudolf J. Freund, Ramon C. Littell,**
and **Lee Creighton** . . . . Order No. A58789

support.sas.com/pubs